DATE DUE

DEC - 7 1998	

BRODART   Cat. No. 23-221

Planning processes
an introduction for geographers

Cambridge Topics in Geography: second series

Editors Alan R.H. Baker, Emmanuel College, Cambridge
Colin Evans, King's College School, Wimbledon

Planning processes
an introduction for geographers

John Herington
Department of Geography, Loughborough University of Technology

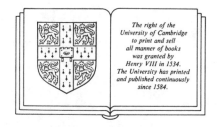

*The right of the
University of Cambridge
to print and sell
all manner of books
was granted by
Henry VIII in 1534.
The University has printed
and published continuously
since 1584.*

Cambridge University Press

Cambridge
New York   Port Chester   Melbourne   Sydney

Published by the Press Syndicate of the University of Cambridge
The Pitt Building, Trumpington Street, Cambridge CB2 1RP
32 East 57th Street, New York, NY 10022, USA
10 Stamford Road, Oakleigh, Melbourne 3166, Australia

First published 1989

Printed in Great Britain at the University Press, Cambridge

British Library Cataloguing in publication data:

Herington, John
Planning processes : an introduction for geographers. – (Cambridge topics in
geography. Second series.)
1. Environment planning. Geographical aspects
I. Title
711
ISBN 0-521-30770-8
ISBN 0-521-31305-8 Pbk

Library of Congress Cataloging-in-Publication Data:

Herington, John.
Planning processes.

(Cambridge topics in geography. Second series)
Bibliography: p.
1. Planning.   I. Title.   II. Series.
HD87.5.H47   1988   361.6   88-2819
ISBN 0-521-30770-8
ISBN 0-521-31305-8 (pbk.)

DS

Contents

Preface

Planning decisions have had wide-ranging consequences for the geography of the developed and developing world. The most direct impact of land-use planning is upon the physical character of settlements, especially the visible form of neighbourhoods, towns, cities, landscapes and regions. But planning also affects people: the daily lives of individual citizens, wherever they live, are influenced by planning decisions. Even economic activity on national and regional scales is circumscribed by government policies.

Because planning is about the organisation of human activity in space it is central to the wider concerns of human geography. The study of 'planning' and 'decision-making' is fast becoming an established and growing component of many A-level geography syllabuses and many first year undergraduate courses at university. However, the subjects are frequently split up into separate topics such as regional policy, regional disparities, urban land use and planning, rural settlement, inner cities, New Towns and so on, making it difficult to grasp the inter-relationship between different aspects of planning and geography.

This book seeks to make in a modest way some connections between the study of planning and the more familiar key themes of human geography. The intention is not to provide a detailed account of planning theory, powers or practice – these are available elsewhere – but to emphasise the broad scope of planning and how the decision-making process changes the geographical patterns and problems the student may observe in the 'real world'. The book emphasises the importance of combining general approaches to the study of planning with case studies on a variety of geographic scales. It draws mainly on the British experience.

I am indebted to the editors of the series and to Peter Walter for particularly helpful and instructive comment during the preparation of the manuscript; my thanks also to Elizabeth Steel and David Evans for their valuable advice. The maps and diagrams were drawn by Ann Tarver in the Department of Geography, Loughborough University.

John Herington
Hathern, Leicestershire

1 Frameworks

The word 'planning' may be used in different ways. In modern society we accept the existence of 'planning' in many spheres of human activity. For example, we talk about planning the economy or educational planning. As individuals we make plans, for example, when we go on holiday we must decide what kind of holiday, how much money we have, where we want to go and how we will get there. In all these cases some form of advance planning is necessary if we are to achieve our objectives. It might be nice to live in a world without planning but most people would find very difficult if they did. A more specialised meaning of 'planning' refers to a way of making an idea work – hence planning a town involves deciding what a town should be like before it is built, where new housing, factories and schools should be located and how they will be built in the time available.

But planning is of course much more than this. It is in effect a form of control over society which seeks to work towards some common good, whether this be the elimination of bad housing or the protection of the countryside. Society needs planners – and the subject of immediate concern to planners is the landscape and settlement patterns society creates. In this sense human geography and planning are closely related. It has even been suggested that 'urban and regional planning is essentially human geography'. Planning and human geography have a lot in common: cities and regions, transport and industry, conservation and resources (see Fig. 1.5). However there is one important distinction: human geography is concerned with the description and evaluation of human activity on Earth whereas planning must look to the future and be concerned with finding solutions to problems.

The study of planning in school for its own sake has hitherto been somewhat neglected, although you have probably studied it under headings like urban geography, settlement geography or economic geography. This book's central focus is that planning is a very important process (distinct from economic or social processes) in moulding the themes which form the core of human geography: places, people and work. The planning process exists within a system consisting of a political organisation (this means central and local government *not* political parties) with power to make decisions, interacting with a political environment which exerts influence on the organisation (Fig. 1.1). The production of plans and controls that we associate with 'planning' (defined below) is the output of the political organisation. There is a complex interplay between professional planners operating in a political organisation and other interest groups (e.g. developers) who make their own decisions and seek to influence planning decision-making in their favour. The planners and other groups often disagree. Fig. 1.1 also emphasises that the study of the planning process is not just how decisions are made but also the results of planning decisions. Decisions have outcomes for space and society which feed back to decision-makers. Planning directly affects areas (regions), points

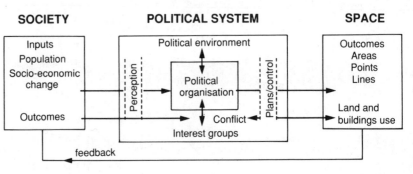

Fig. 1.1 The planning process as a political system. Planning decisions have direct and indirect effects on space and society which in turn affect the way decision-makers respond to change in the political environment. Geographers consider all aspects of the wider relations between politics, planning, space and society.

Source: constructed from ideas contained in Muir, R., 1981, *Modern Political Geography*, London, Macmillan, p.254.

(growth points) and lines (motorways) and brings about change in the use of land and buildings and in turn the economic and social activities of the people who live there. Decision-makers respond to the perceived problems and pressures for action which result from broader structural changes in the economy and society. At times the planning process may be seen as a force causing economic and social change, while at others planning reacts to changes that have already happened.

The chapters in the book are arranged to emphasise these themes. Chapter 2 discusses the decision-making carried out by the political organisations of central and local government. Chapter 3 gives case studies showing how geographical conflict can arise, taking examples from urban and rural environments. Chapter 4 evaluates the geographical outcomes of the planning process. This chapter is divided into three sections, each aims to examine on a progressively broader scale the impact of planning on places, people and work. These examples show the way the planning process activates change on different scales. Finally, it is impossible to ignore modern ideas about how the political system should be changed since these will influence the behaviour of planning organisations in the future. Chapter 5 traces the effect economic recession and political attitudes have had upon planning goals in Britain.

What is planning?

Sometimes referred to as land-use planning, the aim of physical planning is to decide the purpose for which land is to be used in the future and to control the use, layout, design and appearance of buildings. The word 'plan' is rather confusing. It suggests a physical design in the form of a map. But the 'plan' can also include written explanation, statistical projections and financial costings. In addition there can be other forms of planning which do not result in the production of physical plans in the sense of a map e.g. economic and social planning.

The subject matter of physical planning is the same as human geography, namely the built landscape and settlement pattern. But whereas geographers may be content to describe and analyse present and previous patterns of land-use, planners go further and anticipate what pressures and demands will be put on land in the future and how those pressures can be reconciled to achieve a better pattern than the one existing without planning. The idea of physical planning is that through rearranging the uses of land and buildings, settlements and settlement patterns will satisfy public requirements for high standards of design and efficiency.

Physical planning is carried out in many developed countries of the world. In Britain it is often rather misleadingly called 'town and country planning'. Although there are plenty of examples of town planning, both plans for old and new towns, it has to be said that country planning has limited scope. The reason is that most planning controls do not apply to changes taking place in the rural landscape. Farming and forestry are both exempt from planning, although there is some restriction on their activity in National Parks. This is not to say that land-use planning is an unimportant activity in the non-built environment. The physical spread of towns is regulated by planning controls administered by local government authorities. By contrast, changes in the use of rural land are controlled by many other decision-making agencies; for instance, the Ministry of Agriculture, Forestry and Fisheries which controls the future of the farming industry, the State Forestry Commission which makes decisions about the extent of future afforestation and so on. We shall not consider country planning in detail in this book.

It is important to recognise that physical planning is not an end in itself – it is a means to the achievement of social goals. These goals may be the simple ones mentioned above, or they may be broader in scope. The improvement of bad housing conditions, the prevention of social segregation or the reduction in social or spatial differences are all examples of social aims which may underpin physical planning. This kind of planning is in effect, if not intent, a form of social regulation which seeks to bring about certain desired objectives, though it is not often expressed in these terms by professional planners. Inevitably the effects of physical planning decisions go beyond the changing pattern of land-use and buildings we see around us. The 'results' of physical planning are visible but they are also social, economic and political. Economic planning is a particular form of government decision-making concerned with the future progress of the economy, particular industrial sectors and the factors of production (land, labour and capital). In the twentieth century economic planning has become associated with countries having widely different political systems. In the Soviet Union, for instance, there is strong national economic planning with emphasis on five-year plans and, what seems to us in Britain, unduly rigid planning targets for production in different sectors of the economy. The migration of workers is an integral part of this planning which is alien to the developed nations of the western democracies. In these other countries, government controls lay down general guidelines rather than specific directives for the economy.

A further distinction can be made between planning carried out at different geographical levels: for example, national planning for individual countries; regional planning for statistical or administrative divisions of countries, including cities and their hinterlands; and local planning for individual towns or rural areas. Furthermore, different types of government organisation carry out physical and economic planning on national, regional and local scales. In Britain these are respectively central government, the regional offices of central government and semi-official regional groupings of county planning authorities, and the planning departments of local government. There is no regionally elected tier of government.

To add to the confusion, different kinds of planning can be related to the level at which planning is carried out. Thus economic planning is associated with national and regional levels and physical planning with regional and local levels. In practice, planning at one level grades into planning at another and differences are ones of emphasis. Some types of regional plan involve the future spatial arrangement of land. Where new settlements should be sited and how many people and jobs they should contain are matters for regional rather than local planning, as is the question of the scale and location of future public investment in infrastructure (water supply, sewerage, roads). To make matters more complicated, economic and physical planning can take place at both national and local levels. The attraction of industry to particular regions has been a well established role of central government in Britain, but the job of promoting and assembling urban sites for industrial development is falling on local government planning authorities.

For ease of administration some countries have developed strongly hierarchical systems of planning organisation which begin with economic planning controls at the national level and work down to land-use planning controls on a local scale. The differences in planning style even within the countries of Europe are quite marked. In France there is an established history of strong national economic planning, but physical planning is mainly carried out at regional and local levels. The Ministère de l'Equipement prepares national and regional economic plans and co-ordinates the activities of DATAR (the Délégation d'Aménagement du Territoire et d'Aménagement Régional) which deals with national and regional plans for offices and plans for large metropolitan areas, and DAFU (Délégation d'Aménagement Foncier Urban) which administers national urban policy at a regional level. There is no equivalent of this centralised structure in Britain, reflecting a freer approach which governments have taken towards economic planning and the way in which physical planning powers have been decentralised to local government. Some argue that Britain is moving towards a greater degree of centralised planning control, a point taken up in *Chapter 5*.

Summary

We must guard against the danger of using the word 'planning' in a vague and meaningless way without precise definition of the kind of planning involved or the level and type of government organisation. Although it is convenient to separate economic from physical planning, the division between them is not clear cut. Economic planners may seek to promote industrial development in particular urban places and they will be concerned with the spatial impact of their broad economic plans. For instance, the Strategic Plan for North West England sought to promote new industry in the region (economic planning) but restrict the location of new industry to certain areas between Liverpool and Manchester (physical planning). One common element which unifies all kinds of planning at all levels is land. Land may be important both as a factor of production in economic planning or an environmental resource in physical planning. Building on land also changes the social and material environment of different places.

The need for planning

Throughout history, planning has arisen as a 'solution' to perceived social, economic and urban problems. The problems have changed in character as have the solutions. The needs of defence and community well-being prompted the Greeks and Romans to plan the spatial layout and architectural design of their homes, factories and transport routes. The Romans built towns and cities such as London, Bath and Leicester. The Normans built planned fortified towns, for example Flint in North Wales. Indeed, British cities display even today the features of successive generations of architectural and urban planning, from Roman times through the medieval period to the Renaissance and on to the twentieth century (Colin and Rose Bell, 1972).

Planning has been fundamentally important throughout the ages in moulding the physical and social form of cities and regions. Yet why should there have been a move toward planning over the last century? One explanation is that planning was needed for dealing with the intolerable consequences of an uncontrolled free-enterprise economy. The social and economic problems which accompanied the Industrial Revolution were of a different order from anything before and required a social control mechanism – planning. Planning carried out by the State emerged as a desirable and credible alternative to the 'laissez-faire' approach of earlier times.

Government planning was needed to deal with the squalid living conditions found in the industrial cities. The rapid growth of cities in the nineteenth century took place with very little conscious public control over development. Factories were built in places where raw materials and power were available and houses for workers were built close to the industry, often in terraces or back-to-back rows. There was no proper system of government control over such matters as sanitation, both water supply and sewerage disposal, or the density and layout of working class housing areas. Planning, as a 'solution' to these conditions, emerged in the guise of various public health and housing controls.

Firstly, a system of local government control was established – something we take for granted today. Under the 1888 Local Government Act, Counties and County Borough Councils were brought into being to replace the patchy system of municipal boroughs, county and parish government. In 1894 counties were further divided into urban and rural districts, a geographical framework for local administration which remained unchanged until local government reorganisation in 1974. A series of Acts of Parliament were devised to enable these new local authorities to control water supply and sewerage and to regulate the construction of new streets and buildings (the Public Health Act was introduced in 1875) and, rather later, to remove slums (Working Classes Dwelling Act, 1890).

Secondly, the word 'planning' appeared for the first time in government legislation. The broad ranging concerns of modern spatial planning were identified in the Housing and Town Planning Act, 1909. Local authorities were given power to make schemes for developing land 'with the general object of securing proper sanitary conditions, amenity and convenience in connection with the layout and use of the land and of any neighbouring lands'.

The concepts of health, amenity and convenience merged together: thus, not siting houses too close to the glue factory was in the interest of both health, environmental living conditions and convenience; limiting the physical spread of towns to allow inhabitants to be within easy reach of the countryside improved the quality of living conditions (amenity) and kept housing and jobs close together (convenience). In practice, an

5

ideal integration of public health, housing and land-use planning has rarely occurred in the twentieth century. Although most planners are trained to be aware of the links between these separate problems, legislation has been developed in a piecemeal fashion. Nevertheless, the initial concepts of amenity and convenience do provide a framework for understanding many of the early principles which have guided planning in practice (see Table 1.1).

More sophisticated forms of spatial planning became necessary to deal with metropolitan growth. Rises in population led to overcrowding and congestion at the heart of cities and urban sprawl took place in the countryside. Between 1801 and 1851 London's population doubled from approximately 1 million to about 2 million; by 1881 it had doubled again to 4 million and by 1911 it had grown to 6.5 million. Between the two World Wars the pace of urban growth quickened. Increased affluence, cheap housing, improved transport systems and other factors encouraged suburbanisation. Unplanned urban encroachment on the countryside took place and a rapidly rising rate of agricultural land loss reached a peak of 24 000 hectares each year in the mid 1930s. As population moved out into the suburbs journeys to work lengthened, thus increasing traffic congestion. All these trends were greeted with public dismay (Fig. 1.2) and inclined opinion toward central State intervention in land development.

At the same time as the problems of urban growth became evident, long term structural changes in the economy were highlighting the plight of the depressed industrial regions. Regional disparities in unemployment were dramatic during the 1930s. Some form of government intervention, or regional economic planning as it is called today, was needed. During the economic recession of the 1930s central government developed a policy of encouraging industry to move to less prosperous regions which were in need of employment diversification following their dependence on heavy industry; their high levels of unemployment (in contrast to the more prosperous parts of Britain, like south east England) could, it was argued, be reduced by new jobs. Bringing surplus labour into employment would increase the income raised through taxation and reduce payments on unemployment benefit, thus increasing national wealth. If the rate of industrial development could be restricted in the prosperous areas of the country, there would be a better balance in the economy between labour demand and supply. Since the 1930s the State has maintained planning control over industrial land-use and taken an active part in purchasing land for the development of government built industrial estates. Regional policy still exists today, though in a slightly different form.

Physical and economic planning were a reaction to the problems posed by urban and regional change: decay, poverty and congestion in the cities, inequalities of income distribution between groups and regions. Yet it is important to remember that some countries which are experiencing very rapid urban growth still have only embryonic government physical planning systems – Nigeria for instance. Some cities have grown up without any land-use planning and in many places still do. Houston in the USA has no planning or zoning control even though its population growth is expected to occur at 50 000 per annum over the next fifteen years and the sprawl of offices and shopping centres is already causing much public concern. Hence, there can be no unchangeable law which decrees that planning will be needed in all

Table 1.1 Some first principles and modern planning concepts.

Amenity	Living conditions	slum clearance
		comprehensive redevelopment
		self-contained neighbourhoods
		overspill town
	Visual surroundings	housing density
		open space
		Green Belt
		Garden City
Convenience		Land-use zoning
		Industrial estate
		Ring road or by-pass
		Traffic/pedestrian segregation

Fig. 1.2 Humorous view of urban growth in the early twentieth century. The soldiers believed they were fighting to safeguard a rural England whereas the reality was rapid despoliation of the countryside during the inter-war period.

Source: depicted in *Punch* and reprinted as a frontispiece to Williams' Ellis, 1975, *England and the Octopus*, Portmerion, Golden Dragon Books

1914.—MR. WILLIAM SMITH ANSWERS THE CALL TO PRESERVE HIS NATIVE SOIL INVIOLATE.

1919.—MR. WILLIAM SMITH COMES BACK AGAIN, TO SEE HOW WELL HE HAS DONE IT.

places and at all times. Planning will occur where and when society decides that uncontrolled development will give rise to unacceptable social costs and planned rather than unplanned change is preferable (Figs. 1.3 and 1.4). Social costs may be defined as those items which must be paid for by the community rather than the individual – they are sometimes referred to as 'externalities'. Developers impose social costs on others including:

- visual intrusion, pollution, noise;
- infrastructure, in the form of roads, water supply and sewerage;
- clearing rundown property and derelict land;
- providing social services such as education and health.

Ironically, it is public sector developers and nationalised industries that have sometimes imposed the highest social costs – international airports are an example. It is argued that developers of whatever kind ought to be accountable for the costs they impose upon the community at large.

In Britain, it has been widely assumed that an open market for land will not provide an efficient or equitable society and that State direction over future land-use is necessary – assumptions which underpinned the

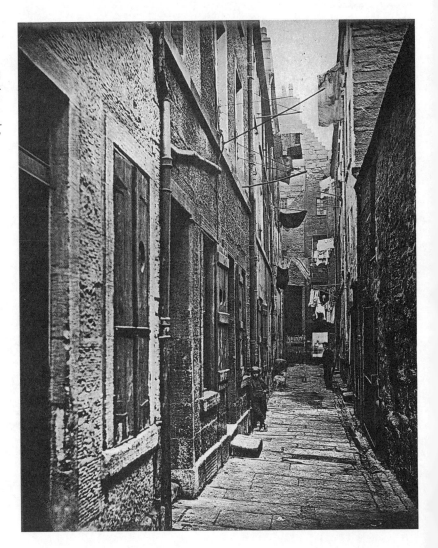

Fig. 1.3 The nineteenth century unplanned industrial city. The narrow dark streets in this view of a Glasgow slum epitomise the squalid social and environmental conditions in which millions lived. Such cities were not planned – they were the result of uncontrolled capitalist enterprise. Out of these circumstances grew the need for the State to provide a decent standard of living and the emergence during the twentieth century of State-controlled urban planning. *Source:* BBC Hulton Picture Library.

Fig. 1.4 The planned New Town was seen as a solution to the problem of overcrowding. People were encouraged to leave the cities and find new homes in better environments outside the city. New Towns offered everything the city could not provide: family housing at a low density in a parkland setting, with all community facilities nearby. This photograph of Crawley New Town shows how the principles of land-use zoning and functional architecture were applied in the post-war period to create a new 'planned' urban landscape very different in character from that shown in Fig. 1.3.
Source: Aerofilms.

popular support for planning in the period between about 1880 and 1945. Only in the 1980s has the case for planning come under attack, a theme taken up in Chapter 5.

Ways of studying planning

Many geographers would agree with Linton's (1957) contention that 'geographers will not be happy in their work unless they can see some relation in its purpose to the current goals of human endeavour and can relate its practice in some way to the needs of the times'. But which needs is geography best fitted to assist? The relationship between planning and the focus of geographical inquiry has varied over time (Willatts, 1971). In the 1940s the need for planning surveys and data collection provided a ready niche for geographers and the importance of both activities should not be underestimated today (Jackson, 1958). In the 1960s and 1970s geographers seemed ideally suited to identify and analyse the problems of urban and regional development and to evaluate pressures on land resources, as illustrated in the work of such geographers as Stamp (1960), Caesar (1964), Wise (1970) and Hall (1974). In the 1970s analysis became more important and advances in statistical techniques enabled geographers to use various models to predict and evaluate the likely outcome of plans (Willatts, 1971). By the 1980s geographers were closely involved in land-use planning and evaluation (Kivell, 1986).

The links between planning and geography have multiplied. Fig. 1.5 attempts to describe the relationship between human geography and the component parts of planning. This relationship depends on two important links:

- (i) they use the same demarcation of fields of study;
- (ii) they have a mutual interest in land resources and human welfare on different scales.

One criticism of the geographers' past contributions to planning is that they have remained aloof from the planning process itself. Yet the geographer needs to understand the importance of planning as a factor in the way places differ and may wish to make judgements about the ability of planning to solve problems. This requires some understanding of the relationship between decisions and geographical outcomes.

The need to place planning as a central theme in urban geography has been emphasised by the British geographer Derek Diamond (1977) in *The UK Space – Resources, Environment and the Future*, p. 482:

'To the traditional geographical factors of site, situation, morphology and function, used in urban geography, must now be added town planning. Indeed, since the impact of town planning on the pattern and function of towns has been cumulative, the total effect . . . is now very substantial indeed. Perhaps it is because planning has been a cumulative process that it has tended to be overlooked by geographers.'

Fig. 1.5 Relationship between the specialisms of planning and geography. The headings are similar and the linking theme is the changing spatial pattern of human activity at different geographical scales.

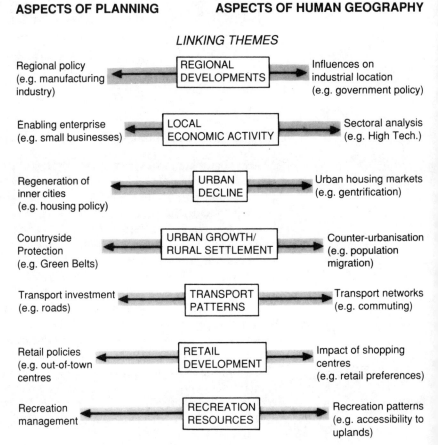

ASPECTS OF PLANNING   **ASPECTS OF HUMAN GEOGRAPHY**

LINKING THEMES

Regional policy (e.g. manufacturing industry) ← REGIONAL DEVELOPMENTS → Influences on industrial location (e.g. government policy)

Enabling enterprise (e.g. small businesses) ← LOCAL ECONOMIC ACTIVITY → Sectoral analysis (e.g. High Tech.)

Regeneration of inner cities (e.g. housing policy) ← URBAN DECLINE → Urban housing markets (e.g. gentrification)

Countryside Protection (e.g. Green Belts) ← URBAN GROWTH/ RURAL SETTLEMENT → Counter-urbanisation (e.g. population migration)

Transport investment (e.g. roads) ← TRANSPORT PATTERNS → Transport networks (e.g. commuting)

Retail policies (e.g. out-of-town centres) ← RETAIL DEVELOPMENT → Impact of shopping centres (e.g. retail preferences)

Recreation management ← RECREATION RESOURCES → Recreation patterns (e.g. accessibility to uplands)

10

Fig. 1.6 Urban planning policies shape the structure of the British city. Planners work to historic patterns of physical and social space. Policy space signifies planning goals formed within a political environment (Fig. 1.1). Actual space represents the visible impact of policy decisions at any one time (e.g. the building of a new shopping centre). The scale, rate and direction of actual change in the city (e.g. as between clearance or preservation of buildings) is thus strongly affected by planning decisions.
Source: adapted from Diamond, D., '*The urban system*' in House, J.W. 1977

Diamond's studies stress the complexity of the relationship between planning and geographical change. Fig. 1.6 shows planning in the form of a 'policy space', both responding to and in turn modifying urban morphology and residential segregation. Planning policy decisions are seen as a response partly to professional ideology and partly to the influence of pressure groups (e.g. conservation societies) which seek to influence policy decisions. The results of planning are visible in the changing built environment of the city.

But as important as the interaction between physical planning and urban geography is the association between economic planning and economic geography. Although the role of government policy is more widely acknowledged as an organisational constraint upon economic

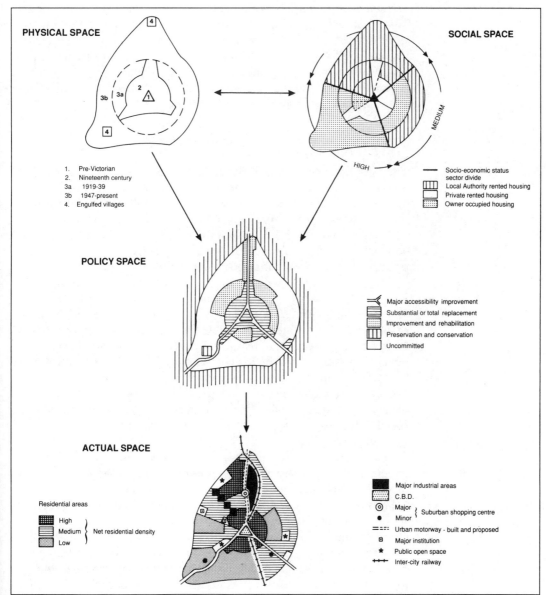

PHYSICAL SPACE

SOCIAL SPACE

1. Pre-Victorian
2. Nineteenth century
3a 1919-39
3b 1947-present
4. Engulfed villages

— Socio-economic status sector divide
Local Authority rented housing
Private rented housing
Owner occupied housing

POLICY SPACE

Major accessibility improvement
Substantial or total replacement
Improvement and rehabilitation
Preservation and conservation
Uncommitted

ACTUAL SPACE

Residential areas
High
Medium } Net residential density
Low

Major industrial areas
C.B.D.
⊙ Major
• Minor } Suburban shopping centre
══ Urban motorway - built and proposed
▣ Major institution
★ Public open space
┼┼┼ Inter-city railway

11

activity there is still a tendency for economic geographers to underestimate the long term influence of government investment on the locational decisions of firms. National economic planning affects the progress of the economy and the expansion or otherwise of particular industrial sectors. Many of the familiar factors which economic geographers refer to in their studies of industrial location are themselves subject to the influence of planning. The availability of good communications is vitally dependent on transport planning decisions (e.g. motorways, airports); the opportunity for factory building depends upon favourable physical planning decisions; even the supply of labour in an area can be linked to the expected growth of population. The combined impact of government policies and physical planning on land-use, settlement, industry and transport is considerable, as well illustrated in the so-called 'M4 Corridor' between London and Bristol (see Chapter 4).

But how do geographers study planning as a subject in its own right? This book suggests a number of key themes. Much must be left out in a selective account. For example, the importance of a sense of planning history is hinted at but there is too little space to study this aspect in depth. Nor do we analyse the influence of rural planning on geographical change which could provide sufficient subject matter for a separate book! Some of the topics are listed below.

(a) The history of planning ideas

The evolution of planning in Britain has been the focus of much literature; see, for instance, Cherry (1974), Hall (1974), Cullingworth (1983) and Ratcliffe (1981). These texts and many others provide an essential context for a more detailed study of the planning process. Each study of planning history reinforces the importance of social context and a need to appreciate the circumstances of the time which brought about new thinking and changes in planning practice.

Physical planning has always involved a complex mix of social vision and political ideology. The built form of the city, as Lewis Mumford (1961) reminds us in *The City in History*, has always reflected the form of its social order. Change the visible form and you also change society. But what kinds of social outcome are worth pursuing? Abolition of poverty, greater control by the community of the private wealth created by development, a more equal society in which all citizens have the opportunity of access to a job and house and the opportunity to live in a decent environment – when these social goals were first announced by social reformers they represented a totally new approach to the organisation of affairs.

Planning thought owes much to the vision of those individuals who saw the social and political possibilities presented by the social control of land ownership. Some enlightened social reformers built model villages for their workers with well laid out houses and open spaces, shopping and community facilities, such as libraries, schools and churches, planned together near the factories; for instance, Salt at Saltaire, Lever at Port Sunlight, Cadbury at Bourneville, and Owen at New Lanark. These planned industrial communities are still visible today and provide rare examples of capitalist planning which influenced the model for later forms of planned New Towns – see Chapter 4.

In a remarkable book called *Garden Cities of Tomorrow*, Ebenezer Howard (1902) gave us a model of how society should be and related it to a model of how geographical change could be planned. Howard argued that the only way to overcome congestion and poverty and the squalor of rural living conditions was to fix a limit to the spread of cities and create entirely new satellite communities, separated from the parent city by a stretch of open country which we now call Green Belt. These new cities would have a finite size of 30 000 population and all the facilities such as jobs, houses and community services, necessary to sustain daily life – indeed they would be self-contained communities. If there was pressure for urban growth this could be accommodated by building more new garden cities linked by public and private transport but separated by Green Belts. The outer metropolitan edges of cities would thus become collections of garden cities which Howard called 'social cities'. The purposes of garden cities was to combine the best countryside and town living – and the concepts guiding the physical development of the city were to be those of health, amenity and convenience.

Howard's utopian view of society was translated into reality. He helped plan and build Letchworth and Welwyn Garden City, north of London and his ideas about the need to contain the growth of cities and decentralise population to deliberately planned new communities was later given substance in the 1944 Abercrombie Plan for Greater London.

(b) Planning regions and organisations

Geographers have long taxed themselves with the problem of how to define regions of value for planning (see for instance Freeman, 1968). A familiar concept has been that of the functional region which comprises separate elements, such as cities, towns and villages, which are functionally dependent on each other in some ways e.g. in commuting trips. The term 'city-region' or 'urban-region' (Geddes, 1915) has come to be the most widely used form of functional region. Geographers have tried to establish the boundaries of functional regions, as in the pioneering studies of Smailes (1944), Green (1966) and Senior (1965), who have been closely involved in the debates about the reform of local government boundaries (see Chapter 2). Unfortunately political convenience has discouraged radical reform of administrative boundaries and the present areas used for plan making and control rarely correspond to the functional regions; this has been a major constraint on effective strategic planning.

The most common difficulties of mismatch arise where the built-up area of towns and cities has extended well beyond their administrative boundaries. Although the post-1974 local government reorganisation overcame this problem in some cases there are many anomalies. In particular, the new administrative divisions do not include the whole sphere of influence of the conurbation (the largest of our continuously built up areas). This meant, for instance, that the West Midlands Metropolitan County Council, which was a strategic planning authority, had to produce a Structure Plan for the conurbation without being able to include in the plan surrounding commuter settlements and other freestanding towns like Tamworth, Stoke-on-Trent and Warwick.

Geographers have also played a formative role in opinions about the appropriate number and size of regions which are larger in scale than the urban region. In *The Provinces of England* the geographer Fawcett (1919) proposed 12 provinces each having a capital and a population of a million, sufficiently large to warrant self-government. Since then there has followed a complex sub-division of Britain into regions of administrative or political significance with ideas about the best solution varying over time as Hall's (1976) useful review illustrates. Today there is still a multiplicity of different spatial frameworks used for planning by different organisations.

Fig. 1.7 A spatial and a functional definition of the city. Conurbations are continuously built-up areas first defined officially in the 1951 Census of Population. The Metropolitan region includes the wider commuting area around the conurbations and other major cities. Which definition is preferable for planning purposes?

Sources: Census of Population, 1966; Centre for Urban and Regional Development Studies, Factsheet 1, December 1983.

(c) Planning as a decision-making process

Studying planning organisations tells us rather little about the process of making planning decisions. As citizens involved in planning issues we may regard these processes as rather secret. Without knowing what is going on we may feel unable to influence decision makers. In practice the decisions of professional planners are made within a framework of laws, government regulations and advice. Policy formulation and tactics may be discussed behind closed doors but day-to-day planning decisions involve a considerable degree of co-operation with developers of land and members of the public, as well as with countless other organisations which planners must consult before making a decision. Moreover, it is the elected representatives on local councils who make the final judgement on planning decisions, based upon the advice given them by the planning officers, except in those cases where the power to make decisions has been delegated to planning officers. A visit to a local planning committee meeting is an instructive way of studying the relationship between officers and members.

In order to understand and, if we wish, influence planning decisions, we need to know something about the way the process operates, its ground rules and the legal constraints within which it operates. The process of plan-making which takes place among planning officials working within a political organisation may be described as a technical model of the planning process – what Peter Hall (1974) has termed 'the making of an orderly sequence of action that will lead to the achievement of a stated goal or goals'. The concept is explained in Fig. 1.8. The process of producing plans is oversimplified by the technical model because at each stage in the decision sequence planners must consult outside interests and members of the public and will be influenced by their views. Nor can each stage be a strictly rational or objective one, since the planner is called to make value judgements: for instance, which alternative plans are the best and which are the worst?

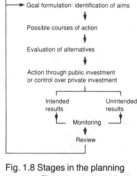

Fig. 1.8 Stages in the planning process. There is no single final decision on land-use, rather a sequence of steps which relate to each other at any one point in time.

(d) The politics of geographical conflict

Keeble (1969) has written that 'planning is the art and science of ordering the use of land and siting of building and communication routes so as to secure maximum practicable degree of economy, convenience and beauty'. But beware of this apparently uncontroversial definition of planning! Can everyone agree on what is an 'acceptable' compromise between development and protection? What is a practicable degree of convenience and beauty? Planning is essentially a form of social control over land-using interests. A planning decision will therefore affect many different groups in society and 'almost any planning decision is to some extent concerned with the allocation of resources so that some people gain while others lose, and for this reason it is misleading, if not downright dangerous, to conceal the overtly political complexion of planning policy' (Roberts, 1981).

Physical planning involves conflict between different groups over the future use of space. It is interesting for the geographer to analyse the nature of these conflicts in the form of case studies which can tell us about the influence each decision maker has on the final planning decision. Case studies may help us to understand the relative power and influence of planners in the political environment. While the technical process of plan-making is interesting, more emphasis is given to the political environment in which struggles over space occur. A model of the political environment can be used to explain the direction and strength of political influence which is brought to bear on planners, for example from developers, environmental lobbies, locally elected representatives (councillors) and politicians (Members of Parliament) – see Chapter 3.

(e) The geographical consequences of planning decisions

The day-to-day operation of planning controls and the way in which they lead to decisions has received less attention from geographers than political scientists – perhaps understandably since these aspects of the planning process are not simply a geographical phenomenon. But do plans work? Do they achieve their aims? For instance, is land being released for development in those locations specified on a plan? If not, what has gone wrong with the plan? Answering these questions is important, firstly, because they tell us about the role of planners in land development and secondly, because the decisions made by planners will have geographical implications. For instance, strong policies to control the spread of housing in the countryside will, if they are successful, reduce the rate of transfer of land from rural to urban use and restrict the spread of towns and cities. As Peter Hall has shown in his book *The Containment of Urban England* (1973) such land-use policies have largely helped avoid the kinds of urban sprawl experienced in some parts of the USA.

It is necessary to look beyond the more obvious physical results of planning decisions to their wider social and political consequences. Since the early 1970s there has been a growing interest among geographers in the evaluation of planning policies and their general consequences for society. Most agree that planning has been a necessary safeguard of the countryside (although not of agricultural landscape change which has been exempt from planning control) but some doubt whether planning has been universally beneficial. Have planning decisions helped to reduce regional differences in prosperity? To what extent have planning decisions been responsible for encouraging the movement of affluent population into the countryside at the expense of the poor, who have been left behind in the inner cities? There are no easy answers to these questions and there is much debate within the planning profession and among academics, about the ability of planning to exert real influence over economic and social change; some regard planning as rather weak, other see planning as a powerful influence (useful accounts in Kirk, 1980; Blowers, 1980). Whatever your own view, an appreciation of the outcomes of planning is clearly relevant to contemporary debate about the causes of our divided society and the problems of regional inequality and inner city decay.

2 Planning decision-making

The organisation of national, regional and local planning is described in this chapter. Various simple models are used to show the network of relationships between different levels of planning, although the descriptions tend to oversimplify the real world of decision-making. In practice planners do not make decisions on their own without reference to wider political or economic influences: for instance, they must listen to the views of developers and pressure groups of various kinds and take into account government policies. These aspects are examined in the next chapter.

As a basis for studying the various kinds of decision-making carried out by government agencies, geographers want answers to the following kinds of questions:

- How is the planning system organised?
- Who makes planning decisions at different geographical levels and what kinds of plan do they produce?
- How do planners seek to influence changing patterns of urban development and how effective are they in doing so?

The number of different kinds of administrative organisation has meant a confusing list of headings for the student. It is easy to become bewildered by the technical language of planning. Yet planning does have its own technical language and a varied terminology in just the same way as do other aspects of human and physical geography.

Descriptive models of the planning system

Many studies of decision-making agencies begin with the activities of central government departments, but planning decisions are made within a broad context of policy-making. Fig. 2.1 suggests the most important policy-making institutions to be those of cabinet, government and Parliament, although important executive decisions are made by the ministerial Departments of State, for example, the Department of the Environment. Individuals and organised pressure groups, collectively called the 'electorate', attempt to lobby politicians in Parliament.

The term 'government' refers to the Prime Minister, the cabinet and the ministerial heads and senior civil servants who advise on and carry out policy. Government will be acutely sensitive to public opinion about contemporary issues including the economy, the environment and the management of the welfare state. Government decides planning policy, but Parliament has the power to approve or modify policy following debate of its merits. Parliament also makes decisions on the siting of large scale development projects, for instance the building of reservoirs, airports or motorways. The decision to abolish the Metropolitan County Councils and the Greater London Council from April 1, 1986 was made by government and approved by Parliament (with far-

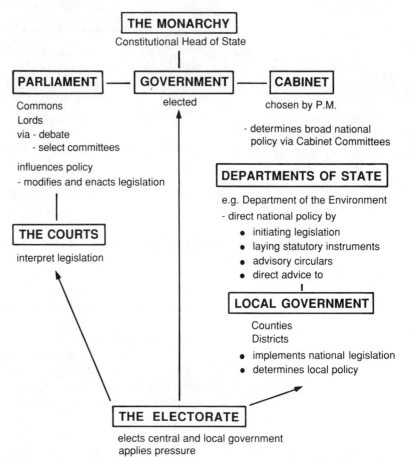

Fig. 2.1 Simple model of the British policy-making system as in 1988. Governments are elected every 5 years and control the executive (Prime Minister and Cabinet), legislature (Parliament) and administration (Whitehall or Central Government Departments). There is local self-government following elections every 3 years. Action about policy issues of national importance, for instance the inner cities, will involve all the institutions shown.

Source: constructed from O'Riordan, T. 'Institutions affecting environmental policy', in Flowerdew, R.(ed)., 1982, *Institutions and Geographical Patterns*, Croom Helm

THE MONARCHY
Constitutional Head of State

PARLIAMENT —— **GOVERNMENT** —— **CABINET**

Commons
Lords
via - debate
- select committees

influences policy
- modifies and enacts legislation

elected

chosen by P.M.

- determines broad national policy via Cabinet Committees

DEPARTMENTS OF STATE

e.g. Department of the Environment
- direct national policy by
  • initiating legislation
  • laying statutory instruments
  • advisory circulars
  • direct advice to

THE COURTS

interpret legislation

LOCAL GOVERNMENT

Counties
Districts
  • implements national legislation
  • determines local policy

THE ELECTORATE

elects central and local government
applies pressure

reaching consequences for the planning of conurbations). Examples of recent parliamentary planning decisions in the field of transport, for example, include the decisions to expand Stansted Airport in Essex and to construct the Okehampton by-pass through a part of the Dartmoor National Park.

It is worth remembering that the influence of Parliament over the direction which planning policy takes is rather limited. Parliament is a debating chamber and not a policy-reviewing institution and much policy is formulated outside Parliament, for instance by Ministers in Cabinet or in their own departments, or in Select Committees which cover the wider aspects of national life which affect land-use planning. These committees influence the views of politicians. The Select Committee on Green Belts and housing land availability, established by the Department of the Environment, is a recent example: it reported in 1984 and took evidence from a number of geographers and planners as well as developers and environmental pressure groups. The Committee expressed its concern about the importance of relaxing Green Belt policy and its views were reflected in a subsequent government circular on Green Belts, (Circular 14/84) published by the Department of the Environment.

The simple description in Fig. 2.1 emphasises the importance of the policy-making institutions within which planning is carried out. Economic and physical planning decisions are made by central and local government and also at the regional level, which is not shown in the figure. In an ideal world it might seem that political organisations would be best structured in a hierarchal fashion: this would certainly be the case with physical planning. National policies would set the framework and these would feed down to the regional and local scales into progressively more detailed plans and projects. The whole process would allow the rational allocation of public resources and their monitoring by central government. The notion of a 'top-down' system of decision-making is outlined in Fig. 2.2.

The model provides a useful starting point for a critical discussion of what is wrong with planning decision-making in Britain. National land-use policy is formulated by the Department of the Environment, but differs from and frequently conflicts with other branches of economic policy; for instance, transport planning, defence planning, industrial location planning and employment planning, which are the responsibility of other central government departments. Moreover, in England and Wales, though to a lesser extent in Scotland, the regional tier is weak or non-existent at present. Nor is planning a highly co-ordinated sequence of responsibilities and decisions as the model suggests would be desirable; rather there is conflict between and within the different levels of planning. National policy will often conflict with local planning policy, for example, where a motorway runs through a locally protected park.

Fig. 2.2 Hierarchal model of government planning – the relationship between national and local levels of decision-making in public sector planning. Each level is constrained by the one above, suggesting a sequence of top-down priorities for land-planning. Compare this with Fig. 1.8 which omits the wider national and regional context.

Source: Bruton, M.J. and Nicholson, D.J., 1985 'Strategic land-use planning and the British development plan system'. *Town planning Review*', vol 56, no. 1, Fig. 1.

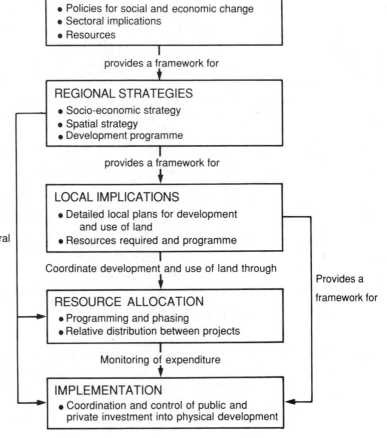

National planning

Economic and physical planning at the national level is carried out by a number of different decision-making organisations. These are the central government departments, each headed by a Minister of State, which are responsible for producing and supervising the implementation of policies, all of which directly or indirectly affect patterns of regional and urban development:

Department of the Environment
- physical (land-use) planning carried out by local authorities;
- housing;
- inner cities;
- New Towns and Urban Development Corporations;
- countryside planning, environmental protection and water supply;
- local government and the administration of council finances.

Department of Transport
- road, rail and air infrastructure;
- building motorways and trunk roads and supervising the allocation of grants to local authorities (County Councils) for local spending on roads;
- Channel Tunnel.

Department of Trade and Industry
- industrial regeneration;
- manufacturing and service industries;
- high technology;
- the location of industrial development through regional policies and the Regional Development Grant.

Department of Employment
- Employment and training policy;
- economic planning, small businesses, development of tourism;
- Manpower Services Commission – responsible for employment centres and mobility of labour.

Department of Energy
- investment plans of nationalised industries;
- siting of nuclear power stations;
- oil drilling installations;
- coal mining developments.

Ministry of Defence
- location and size of service bases, reservation of training grounds;
- research establishments.

Ministry of Agriculture, Fisheries and Food
- farm prices and crop support quotas, upland hill farm subsidies;
- reclamation of moorland and lowland.

In addition to the main departments, a variety of different government agencies have an interest in planning. These are known colloquially as quangos or 'quasi-autonomous non-governmental organisations'. While they may be established for a particular purpose they have no power to alter policies. The Countryside Commission is a good example. Since 1972 the Commission has been an independent department, having formerly been under the Department of the Environment. It plays an important role in national countryside and rural planning, having powers under the Countryside Act, 1968, to designate National Parks and Areas of Outstanding Natural Beauty, and manage public access to the countryside (see Table 2.1 and Fig. 2.3)

The Department of the Environment, formed in 1970, is the one department which has single responsibility for many aspects of physical planning and development. However, despite the DoE's wide ranging responsibilities in land-use planning, infrastructure development and public expenditure, not every aspect of national life that influences planning is decided by the DoE. The DoE is also a cumbersome organisation containing a number of sub-departments not all of which are directly concerned with physical planning. The complexity of the divided responsibilities within the DoE perhaps explains why the production of an integrated national plan for land-use has never been attempted. The 1964 Labour Government published a 'National Plan' in 1965 but this document hardly touched on spatial planning issues.

Regional planning

Governments have often shown little interest in regional planning, preferring most decisions to be made nationally or locally. However, most central departments have decentralised their activities to regional offices which are sometimes called 'arms of Whitehall'. Their job is to co-ordinate the work of the different departments in the regions. Although there is no nationally agreed physical plan, there have been different kinds of regional planning produced at various times.

During the early/mid 1960s the then Department of Economic Affairs published a number of regional economic development studies (e.g. The North West: a regional study, 1965). Of more interest to geographers were the 'regional strategic plans' published in the early 1970s by the Economic Planning Councils (e.g. The Strategic Plan for the South East, 1971). They involved a three-way arrangement for decision-making between civil servants from the Department of Environment, the Economic Planning Councils and local planning officials. In some regions like the North West special teams of geographers and planners were brought together to prepare these strategies. Each strategic plan attempted to show in diagrammatic form the proposed location of desired future urban growth (Fig. 2.4). The strategies had a dual role: on the one hand they offered a spatial framework for the economic and investment decisions of central government and large development interests and on the other they provided some rather general guidance for local planning. The strategic plans formed guidelines rather than policy and the policies in them have become out-of-date and today are largely irrelevant outside the South East. House's useful (1977) analysis showed the strategies often had mutually conflicting aims and simply reflected the established political interests of the different local authorities; notwithstanding this criticism, each strategy contains a range of data and analysis which warrants geographical investigation today.

Table 2.1 The extent of designated land resources in England and Wales. Although all such land is the responsibility of central government it is usually defined by local planning policies (e.g. the detailed boundaries of Green Belts). New building is strictly controlled in these locations but the re-use of existing buildings may be accepted.

	Number	Area (km²)	% National land
AONBs*	35	14 490(+)	12
National Parks	10	13 600	9
Heritage coasts	35	1 084 (linear km)	26 (of coastline)
SSSIs†	3041	7 913	5
Agricultural land (grades 1 and 2)	—	20 210	14
Green Belts	13	17 610	12

*AONB – Area of Outstanding Natural Beauty
†SSSI – Site of Special Scientific Interest

Source: Solesbury, W., 1986, 'Safeguarding nationally important land resources', in K.G. Willis, *Contemporary Issues in Town Planning*, Aldershot, Gower.

Fig. 2.3 Nationally safeguarded conservation and recreation areas in England, Wales and Scotland. The aim is to preserve and enhance natural beauty and promote public enjoyment. In Environmentally Sensitive Areas (ESAs) farmers are grant-aided to conserve the visual appearance of the landscape and protect flora and fauna.

Source: Countryside Commission, 1988.

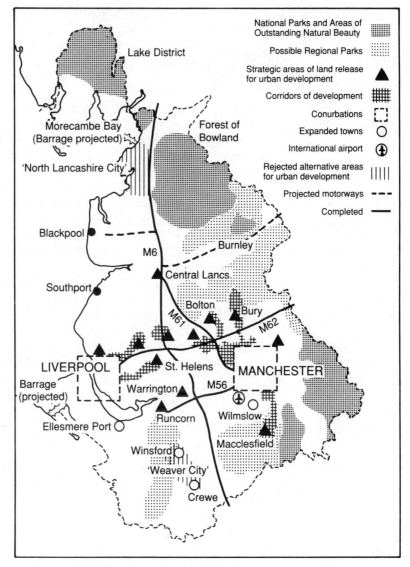

Fig. 2.4 Basic elements of a strategic regional plan published in the 1970s. The most important national and regional policies are indicated in diagramatic form. Strategic plans of this kind have no legislative authority. County and District authorities can exercise their planning powers in the way they see fit.

Source: based upon North West Joint Planning Team, 1974 *Strategic Plan for the North West*, HMSO.

Local Planning

In England and Wales local planning is carried out by 47 County Councils and 369 District Councils created under the 1972 Local Government Act. In Scotland it is carried out by 6 Regional Councils and 37 District Councils.

The present structure of local government follows a history of reforms which began with the 1888 Local Government Act, a piece of legislation which Cullingworth (1982) referred to as 'that fatal separation of town and country into watertight compartments'. There have been a number of suggestions. The Royal Commission on Local Government in England (Redcliffe-Maud Commission) which reported in 1969, proposed that with a few exceptions local planning should be carried out by 58 all-purpose unitary authorities defined largely on the basis of travel-to-work hinterlands. The proposed exceptions were Merseyside, Greater Manchester and the West Midlands where planning would be carried out on two scales – Counties and Districts. Many geographers argued at the time that it made sense to base new areas of planning administration on the urban centres and the areas influenced by them, but the 1972 reform of local government rejected the unitary principle in favour of the present two-tier system of Counties and Districts, drawing a distinction between Metropolitan (essentially the conurbations) and non-Metropolitan Counties and Districts. As shown in Fig. 2.5, the position of large cities such as Plymouth, located in non-Metropolitan counties, is virtually the same after as before reform. Sadly only a small number of the newly created Districts contain complete travel-to-work areas. Plymouth's commuting field extends over neighbouring Districts in Cornwall and overlaps the adjacent county of Devon.

As a result of the Local Government Act of 1972 the ideal of strategic and detailed planning being the responsibility of one administrative authority was abandoned. The strategic (structure) and detailed (local) planning functions were assigned instead to the new County and District authorities respectively. This opened the way to strategic and detailed planning being performed by elected bodies with different political complexions, aims and planning powers. The Counties became responsible for the Structure Plans and the Districts for Local Plans (which are explained on page 00). Not surprisingly, there are calls today for a further reform of the organisation to achieve a more sensible division of effort between the various levels of planning.

In 1986 the government abolished the Metropolitan Counties and the Greater London Council because they were thought to be an unnecessary tier of government. Their planning functions have been taken over by the Districts which will act individually to produce unitary development plans or through a system of jointly elected boards. The two-tier system remains in the non-Metropolitan Counties.

Fig. 2.5 (a) (b) The impact of local government reform on Plymouth. Local government reform under the English Royal Commission (Redcliffe-Maud) proposals of 1969 suggested a single tier unitary authority covering Plymouth and surrounding commuting hinterland (a). This would have overlapped the adjacent counties of Devon and Cornwall. In contrast, the 1972 Local Government Act introduced a two tier system of Counties and Districts with commuting hinterland replaced by four separate Districts (b).

Sources: Royal Commission on Local Government in England 1966–1969.

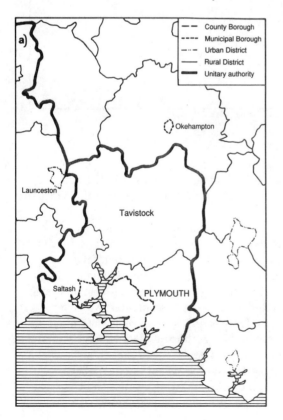

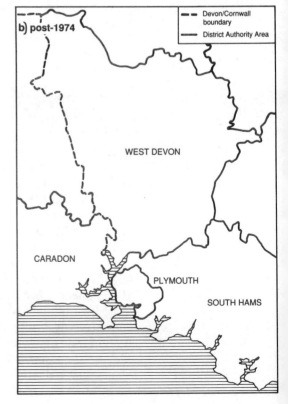

National–local planning relationships

The danger with breaking the organisation of planning down into a hierarchy of national, regional and local levels is that it implies only a 'top-down' relationship of powers. Is this true? There is much interaction and negotiation between central and local government departments and their respective agencies at different levels in the system. Some aspects of central–local relationships are examined using two alternative models.

1. The 'top-down' model   assumes central government determines national policy and local government planners put it into effect. While there is no national land-use plan in England and Wales, in the sense of a map which shows what each piece of land is to be used for, there are national policies. In 1977 the Scottish Development Department published some 'national planning guidelines' for Scotland, seen in Fig. 2.6, which showed what kinds of economic development could be acceptable to central government in different locations and thus effectively form the basis of a national land-use policy.

There are other examples of strong central government influence over land-use and the economy: road building is planned by the Department of Transport; countryside policy is administered by the Countryside Commission and the Ministry of Agriculture, Forestry, Fisheries and Food; special development organisations are established by the Department of the Environment e.g. New Towns, under the 1946 New Towns Act, Urban Development Corporations under the

Fig. 2.6 National planning guidelines in Scotland. The map is not binding on any decision-making authority but acts as a guide for developers and landowners seeking to promote rural development schemes. An interesting example of how central government has anticipated the conflicts between industry and conservation rather than leaving this solely to local decision-making.

Source: Scottish Development Department, 1977.

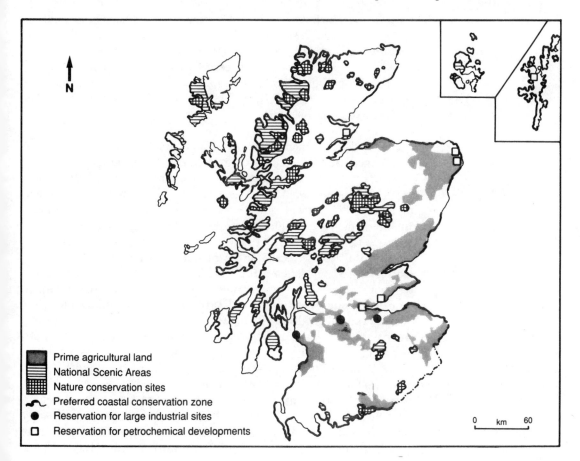

Prime agricultural land
National Scenic Areas
Nature conservation sites
Preferred coastal conservation zone
Reservation for large industrial sites
Reservation for petrochemical developments

0   km   60

25

1980 Planning and Land Act and by the Development Commission set up by the Department of Trade and Industry; careful budgetary control of local government spending is carried out by the Department of the Environment.

In three other important respects the Department of the Environment exerts strong control over local planning authorities' actions:

(a) DoE supervises the preparation and review of Structure Plans and is responsible for approving them, as well as ensuring that both Structure and Local Plans conform to the regulations and that local authority investment plans are realistic.

(b) DoE intervenes directly in the day-to-day planning decisions only when there are disputes between prospective developers and the local authority over whether to grant or refuse planning permission. A developer may object to or appeal against a local planning authority which refuses planning permission and the Secretary of State may grant planning permission after a public inquiry even though the local authority has refused it. The power of the Secretary of State to make decisions on these planning appeals obviously affects local planners who may be unwilling to refuse permission if they think the DoE will uphold an appeal. The Secretary of State thus has strong powers to control the uses to which particular parcels of land are put, at least on those occasions when planning permission is refused by the local planning authority (see appeal sites in Fig. 2.7).

(c) DoE may 'call-in' any planning application, not just those that are refused, which are considered strategically significant and might lead to a departure from the approved local authority plan. A public inquiry must be held and the decision of the Secretary of State is final. Several big and controversial development projects have been decided in this way, for example, the National Coal Board's proposal to mine coal near the Vale of Belvoir, which is discussed in the next chapter.

2. The 'bottom-up' model   stresses the power of Counties and Districts to influence national planning control. Local authorities are given considerable discretion in making local planning policy: it is they who decide what issues should be considered in a plan and they who have to implement the plan with developers. Although the Secretary of State can intervene when conflicts arise, it is the District planners who are entirely responsible for controlling, on a day-to-day basis, which developments receive planning permission and which are refused. The Secretary of State's function is to co-ordinate the different plans of the local councils to ensure that their development plans and development control procedures are in line with broad national planning policies. Because central government sets the legal limits it is inevitably drawn into day-to-day local planning decisions. National planning policies are written in very general terms which gives local planners considerable leeway over how they are to be interpreted. The working and requirements of planning legislation are explained to local authorities by statutory instruments (which have the force of Acts of Parliament), departmental circulars (which are advisory) and bulletins; but these cannot provide guidance for every planning case. Specific proposals are considered 'on their merits' within a framework of principles which may change over time. All of which makes it very difficult to say that central government plays the dominant role in planning decision-making.

However, local politics is a great influence on planning decisions and may sometimes help to change the mind of central government. The emphasis given to national policy and the degree of unwillingness to comply characterises local power. Liverpool City Council's resistance, in common with some other local authorities, to the government's reduction in the block grant in 1985–6, is an example of 'bottom-up' relations. Another instance of local resistance took place when the Department of the Environment produced draft new guidance for planning in green belts. There was outcry from some Tory-controlled Counties which helped to bring a change of direction in policy.

Summary

Sometimes it appears that planning decisions are made at national level and the local planners have little say in the outcome; on other occasions changes in planning seem to come from the local level. Much decision-making takes the form of a partnership, with neither level dominating. Perhaps the best known attempts at partnership in an official sense are the seven Inner City Partnership authorities set up under the Inner Urban Areas Act of 1978. They brought together central and local government with chambers of commerce and voluntary organisations in an attempt to revitalise the economies of the inner cities.

But it is important not to forget that behind the formal organisation of planning lies Parliament and the complex interweaving of planning with political ideals on national and local scales. Central government is called to play an increasingly important role in the management of local finance as Bennett's (1982) research shows. For any government determined to reduce the role of the State in public spending, it is obvious that local government will be a target. For this reason alone the 'top-down' model appears to provide quite a good explanation for contemporary central–local interaction.

The control of change by local planning

Under Town and Country planning legislation, Counties and Districts are required to produce plans which seek to control the future pattern of urban development. The plans are usually in the form of maps or diagrams. Because the purpose of a Structure Plan is to establish general policy for future change in the planning area i.e. County administrative unit, it is not important to show how planning proposals relate in any detail to individual plots of land. Structure Plan key diagrams are usually brightly coloured and diagrammatic in style, with the policies indicated approximately to scale but without an Ordnance Survey base, as shown in Fig. 2.7. In contrast, Local Plans are intended to show how Structure Plan policies are interpreted in more detail at the scale of individual settlements, especially where rapid change is taking place. Fig. 2.7 shows how Structure Plans are translated into Local Plans. It also illustrates that development pressures and central government decisions may lead to sites being released that were not intended in the plan, thus upsetting the logic of the County–District hierarchy of plan-making.

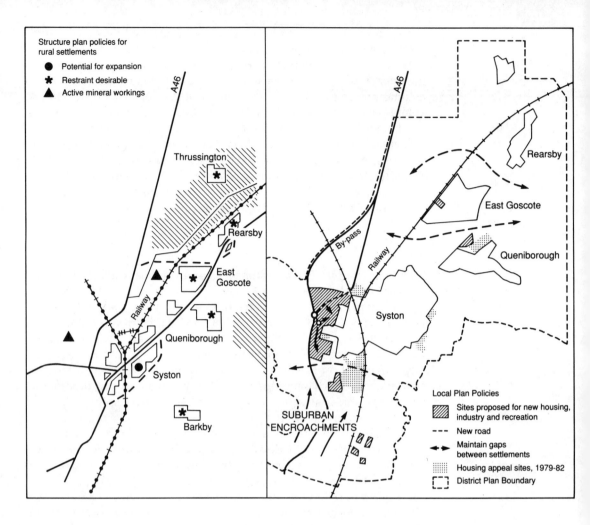

Structure plan policies for rural settlements
● Potential for expansion
✳ Restraint desirable
▲ Active mineral workings

Local Plan Policies
▨ Sites proposed for new housing, industry and recreation
--- New road
◄—► Maintain gaps between settlements
▒ Housing appeal sites, 1979-82
⌐¬ District Plan Boundary

Fig. 2.7 Local government policies for managing land-use change on the urban fringe. The different roles of Structure and Local Plans are revealed in these plans for the Wreake Valley, north east of Leicester. The Local Plan may still prove difficult to implement because developers are allowed by Central Government to build on sites not allocated for development in the plan.

Source: Leicestershire County Council, 1987.

Local Plan maps must show physical relief features and the location of specific sites. However, there are three types of Local Plan and the presentation differs somewhat:
- **District Plans** cover fairly large areas such as a small town or collection of rural settlements. These plans may be diagrammatic and cover essentially the same subjects as the Structure Plan but the proposals are specific to a certain site and shown at a scale of 1:25000.
- **Action Area Plans** identify quite small areas, residential neighbourhoods or shopping centres for instance, which need major redevelopment or renewal over a ten year period. The maps show detail often at a scale of 1:2500.
- **Subject Plans** cover particular topics which Counties and Districts think require some special investigation, for example: green belts, the rural-urban fringe, recreation, mineral extraction, reclamation and waste disposal.

All these types of Local Plan are ideal sources of information for local geographical studies. Copies should be available in the central reference libraries of the appropriate local authority or in the planning department of the local authority themselves.

Structure Plans

The procedure for preparing Structure and Local Plans is laid down in planning Acts and statutory instruments. The first step is to make a geographical survey of the County or District area for which the plan is being prepared. This covers many aspects of interest to geographers including land-use changes, population trends, economic trends, transport networks and so on. The purpose is not to gather information for its own sake but rather to build up an impression of the key problems or issues requiring a planned 'solution'. The different subjects treated by a Structure Plan include: population, settlement, employment, industry, housing, retail, transport, conservation, leisure and recreation, minerals.

Having identified the main problems requiring attention under each subject heading, the County planners must decide what policies are desirable to solve them, and give guidance on the future direction of development. The emphasis given to particular solutions will vary according to which problems the planners consider to be important. In rural 'Shire' counties bordering the major cities of Britain a familiar solution to urban growth has been to restrain the overall future levels of economic and population activity and steer development away from environmentally important areas. With the effects of economic recession being felt even in these traditionally prosperous areas, these policies are being reviewed (see Chapter 5).

In the course of preparing Structure and Local Plans planning officers must consult individuals and interested organisations in the community at various stages. The public have a right to be consulted at the first stage – the definition of problems and key issues – and to give their views on the kind of planning solutions favoured by the planners. Once the preparation of a Structure Plan is completed it is submitted officially to the Secretary of State for the Environment who will usually arrange for an 'Examination in Public' (EIP) to be held into any major controversial issues. Only those groups or individuals invited to attend by the Department of the Environment are allowed to participate at the EIP. The process whereby planners publish draft plans, consult the public for their views, modify the plans, consult the public again and so on can last many months. The time taken to prepare plans has been a source of criticism.

Are Local Plans effective?

Local planning involves more than the production of plans, important though these are. There would be little purpose to plan-making if there were no agencies able to carry out the development proposals. The Local Plan indicates where the local authority would like to see particular kinds of development take place, such as the allocations of land and thus shows potential builders or developers where they might expect planning permission to be approved or refused. However the relationship between Structure and Local Plans and the day-to-day control of urban development is less direct than might be expected.

Developers will apply for permission to develop sites which are not shown on a District plan and still hope to get approval. For example, a high proportion of planning permissions for housing are given for developing land which is not allocated for that purpose on a plan. It is worth noting the figures shown in Table 2.2 based upon data obtained for the West Midlands. The table shows that 71.6% of all applications were for residential development on land not allocated for housing. When land actually released is compared to land applied for, the success rate of these applications was only 13.1% compared with the much higher figure of 53.3% on allocated land, as might be expected. Interesting questions are raised by this analysis: why did developers think they stood a chance of getting permission on land not shown in plans? And why should a relatively high proportion (38.3%) of these 'rogue' applications have been successful?

Firstly, planning applications are decided with regard to 'all material considerations' of which the Structure or Local Plan is but one, albeit in theory a major one. Highway and traffic requirements, design and density and the desire to make sure the new development does not obtrude into the landscape are other factors which the planning officers and their committee of elected representatives must take into account before deciding whether to refuse or grant permission. If the Structure or Local Plan policies are too vague to be helpful, or no plan exists, the application will have to be judged on its merits.

Secondly, economic pressures may prove difficult to resist even if there are planning policies restricting urban development. This is particularly true of land on the edge of towns and villages which is sought after for commuter housing but is not located within a Green Belt. Individual applications may be permitted, making it difficult to prevent gradual urbanisation of an area. Fig. 2.8 provides us with an interesting insight into the spatial impact of development pressures on the fringes of Reading and Wokingham. At first glance it might be thought that most of the locations under greatest pressure for housing are those where planning policies have been upheld, especially the gap between Reading and Wokingham and the indeterminate ribbon development between Wokingham and Crowthorne. But an examination of the 'success' rate of individual planning applications, also shown in Fig. 2.8, shows that the percentage of approvals is relatively high in several urban fringe locations, for example immediately west of Wokingham. This analysis tells us nothing about the number of dwellings approved, nor the area of permissions granted,

Table 2.2 Expectation and reality in land development decisions.
The gross area of land (in hectares) subject to a planning application compared to land released as a result of a planning permission. Developers are much more successful on land proposed for development in a plan (column 1) but try to gain permission for a much larger land area not shown on plans (column 2). Data refers to part of the West Midlands, 1968–73.

	Allocated on Development Plan for		
	housing	non-housing	Total
Planning application submitted (ha)	621.0 28.4%	1565.7 71.6%	2186.7 100%
Land released for development (ha)	331.0 61.7%	205.4 38.3%	536.4 100%
Permission success rate	53.3%	13.1%	24.5%

Source: Joint Unit for Research on the Urban Environment, 1977, *Planning and Land Availability*, Birmingham, University of Aston, p.50

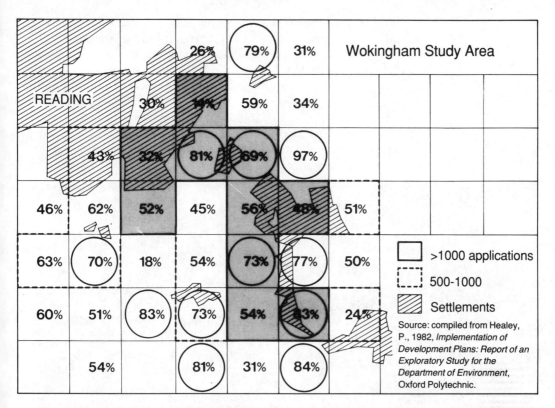

Wokingham Study Area

READING

| >1000 applications |
| 500-1000 |
| Settlements |

Source: compiled from Healey, P., 1982, *Implementation of Development Plans: Report of an Exploratory Study for the Department of Environment*, Oxford Polytechnic.

Fig. 2.8 Local authority planning decisions in the Wokingham/Reading area of Central Berkshire, 1974–80. Analysis of planning applications and refusals reveals degrees of constraint and permissiveness in planning control in a non-Green Belt location. The gaps between settlements have been protected and refusals have been high in some of the areas where pressure for housebuilding is greatest. However, in some other areas between 440 and 480 out of every 1000 applications have been permitted.

only the total number of applications (see Fig. 2.9). Nonetheless, high 'success' rates are likely to indicate considerable housing development in those locations where the number of applications is high.

Thirdly, although urban development proposals may not accord with

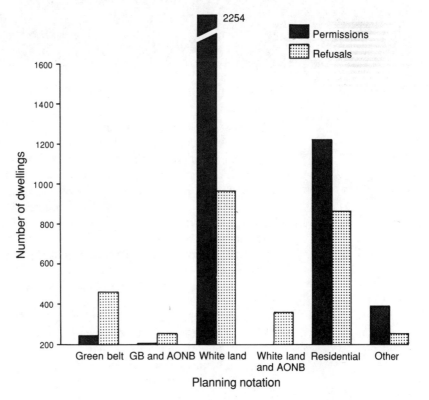

Fig. 2.9 Local planning decisions in High Wycombe, 1974–80. Number of dwellings refused under six different kinds of planning policy. Most proposals in Green Belts and AONBs are turned down. In contrast, 2254 dwellings were allowed on land having no special planning purpose ('White land'), double the amount of dwellings permitted on land having a clear residential allocation in plans (compare with Table 2.2).

Source: as Fig. 2.8

31

general planning policy for an area, they may meet the requirements of a national government and thus still receive approval. A relatively high proportion of 'non-allocated' land development may receive approval from the Department of the Environment following a planning appeal and public inquiry; such developments may have very significant spatial impact on land development and on the appearance and social function of settlements (see Fig. 2.10 and Fig. 2.7). Developers are often able to demonstrate at planning inquiries that the general policies contained in Structure and Local Plans do not apply to their sites or that granting permission will not contradict planning goals.

Fig. 2.10 A public inquiry in action. This view of the inquiry into the CEGB's proposed Sizewell 'B' nuclear power station emphasises the formal nature of the decision-making procedures. The proponents and opponents with their professional advisers face each other across the floor and the Government-appointed Inspector sits on the platform.
Source: East Anglian Daily Times.

Summary

The distinction between general plans and the day-to-day decision-making in planning is not as obvious as it sounds. It is perhaps not surprising that some commentators of the planning process are sceptical about the effectiveness of plans. One difficulty is that the translation of general policies into specific site developments is carried out by two separate planning authorities: the Counties, who produce Structure Plans, and the Districts, who prepare most Local Plans and carry out development control. The problem of implementing plans arises in part from the complex world of decision-making which takes place outside planning offices. Most planning decisions involve difficult choices: between allowing development or refusing it, between protecting the environment or increasing jobs. Developers, individuals and the community all have opinions and expect to have a say in these choices. Planners must try to balance private interests against society's needs. A study of planning decision-making makes us aware of the need for all of us to make judgements about aesthetic and social issues as they relate to people and the environment.

3 Geographical conflict: some case studies

Planners are often hated and loved: hated when they stop us doing what we want and loved when they protect us from somebody else doing something we don't like. Planning conflicts arouse fierce controversy and their resolution involves difficult value judgements. On the one hand it is important to preserve the individual's freedom to do as he or she wishes and on the other there is a need for society to control change for the benefit of the majority. How can conflicts be studied in a relatively neutral way by geographers?

The resolution of planning conflicts takes the form of a game in which various players come together with the purpose of winning. The game begins whenever conflict of interest arises, for instance when a plan proposes a change in land-use. The siting of new houses or roads may, for example, be opposed by local residents, or plans for a new shopping complex in a historic town centre may anger conservationists. How is the game played? Each player has a different set of values and attitudes about the future and will bring pressure to bear on opponents to influence the outcome. The players must use the rules governing planning decision-making outlined in the last chapter, that is, they must act within the framework of institutions, legislation and operating practices which make up the planning system.

In this chapter examples of land-use conflict are taken from the inner cities, the urban–rural fringe and the countryside. First, the key players are explained and their inter-relationship is analysed using a simple model of the political environment.

Players in the decision game

Most conflicts over the future use of land involves three main kinds of player – developers, environmental groups and planners.

(a) Developers

Developers can be classified into the various groups listed in Table 3.1. Private sector developers are primarily interested in maximising profits from a scheme. The public sector does not usually undertake development only for financial motives but rather to fulfil duties and functions set down by statute. Local authorities may pursue various policy aims (e.g. economic development) rather than financial return. Increasingly the financing of urban development projects takes the form of a partnership between private and public sources, with building societies, banks and pension funds in conjunction with local authorities and grants supplied by central government, as illustrated in Fig. 3.1.

Public developers generate demands for very large areas of land (e.g.

for motorways) and these projects can become the source of major planning conflict. At times public agencies develop a split personality in their approach to resolving land-use conflict. For instance, the Department of Transport, a central government agency, is required to operate as both planner and engineer insofar as it plans the programme of motorways and supervises the actual construction of roads. The public will often oppose the route of new roads if their peace and quiet or a view of attractive countryside is threatened. In such cases the Departments of Transport and the Environment will have to hold planning inquiries into their own engineering schemes. Similarly, a District Council may require planning approval from its own

Table 3.1 Classification of developers and their land interests. Public sector developments may require extensive land areas in countryside locations, thus creating the potential for conflict with environmental interests.

Developers	Role in process	Land interests and objectives
Private		
Property companies and housebuilders	Entrepreneurs seeking to coordinate or undertake development	Maximise profits. Volume housing, retail centres
Financial institutions, insurance companies, pension funds, banks	Supply development and investment funding for property development	Aim to match liabilities with appropriate investments. Regional centres, science parks
Industrial companies	Construction ICI BNF (British Nuclear Fuels) BT (British Telecom)	Dependent on profits in long-term but otherwise short-term provision of service: financial return; diversification to reduce risks. Nuclear power, tele-communications
Public		
Statutory undertakers Regional Water Authorities Central Electricity Generating Board Dept. of Transport	Infrastructure provision (highways, gas, electricity, drainage, water supply and sewerage)	Fulfil duties and functions as given in legislation. Undertake development to meet own requirements. Motorways, reservoirs, power stations
Public development agencies UDC Development agencies HIDB FC	Undertake/facilitate development in accordance with policy initiatives	Again aim to fulfil duties and functions as set by statute; more direct interest than statutory undertakers in progressing development. Afforestation, airports, rail
Local authorities as developers	Undertake or facilitate development	In relation to wider statutory roles (e.g. as housing authority) leading to development needs/ requirements, or in pursuit of other policy aims (e.g. economic development) rather than financial return *per se*. Housing, industry.

Source: adapted from Bruton, M. and Nicholson, D., 1987, *Local Planning in Practice*, London, Hutchinson, Table 8.1

department's officers before it can develop its land for factory building.

Developers lobby politicians and planners to bring about the changes they desire. The House Builders Federation is a good example of a developers' pressure group which has effectively pressed central government to relax planning controls as they affect residential development (see Fig. 3.2).

(b) Environmental pressure groups

Environmental pressure groups consist of individuals who band together to fight the schemes proposed by developers or planners. A

Fig. 3.1 Partnership between private and public sources of finance to solve urban problems. The money is being used to regenerate a run-down peripheral overspill housing estate on Merseyside. *Source:* Town and Country Planning Association Summer School, February 1985.

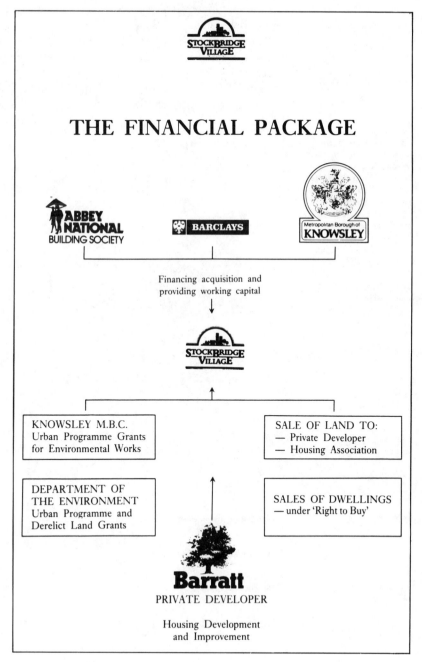

35

distinction has been made by Short (1986), based upon research in Central Berkshire, between 'stoppers', who want to protect their physical environment and 'getters', who want to see community life improved by the provision of new facilities. Both groups appear to have a short life-cycle, coming together to fight a project and then disappearing when the battle is over. However, it is important to remember that local authorities can also behave in the manner of 'stoppers'. Fears about the environmental, social and financial consequences of overspill (the planned movement of population out of the cities) have led many rural County Councils to oppose urban expansion in their areas (Fig. 3.3).

There are other kinds of nationally recognised pressure groups with a total membership of perhaps three million. National pressure groups like the Council for the Protection of Rural England (CPRE), the County Landowners Association (CLA) or National Farmers' Union (NFU) seek to protect the countryside against urban encroachment (Lowe and Goyder, 1983). In the urban environment the Civic Trust, founded in 1957, promotes high quality architecture and planning and opposes development thought to be ugly or out of place. The role of

Fig. 3.2 Attitudes to new housebuilding in south east England. A survey carried out by MORI on behalf of the House Builders Federation. Opinions toward new housebuilding in the respondents' locality vary by sex, age and political allegiance, suggesting a more positive view of change than the popular image.

Source: New Houses Marketing Board, 1987.

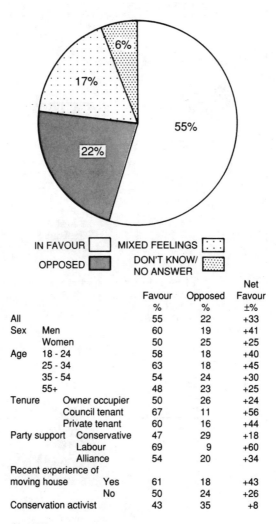

		Favour %	Opposed %	Net Favour ±%
All		55	22	+33
Sex	Men	60	19	+41
	Women	50	25	+25
Age	18 - 24	58	18	+40
	25 - 34	63	18	+45
	35 - 54	54	24	+30
	55+	48	23	+25
Tenure	Owner occupier	50	26	+24
	Council tenant	67	11	+56
	Private tenant	60	16	+44
Party support	Conservative	47	29	+18
	Labour	69	9	+60
	Alliance	54	20	+34
Recent experience of moving house	Yes	61	18	+43
	No	50	24	+26
Conservation activist		43	35	+8

(N=1100)

both rural and urban groups is to pressure Ministers, to educate the public about threats to the environment and to stimulate local debate about the environmental consequences of planned change. Rural pressure groups have had varying success in opposing some well known developers' projects, such as the British Airport Authority's proposals for the Third London Airport at Stansted and (successfully) British Coal's plans to mine from three sites near the Vale of Belvoir. The Civic Trust successfully put pressure on Ministers to bring in legislation controlling urban change in Conservation Areas under the Civic Amenities Act, 1957 and it has played an influential role in the protection and enhancement of town centres. The Town and Country Planning Association (TCPA), formed in 1899 as the Garden Cities Association, is a very lively pressure group for planning and lobbying Parliament on many aspects of general and detailed planning matters. It believes in the concept of planned decentralisation, outlined in Chapter 1.

Fig. 3.3 East Hertfordshire's perception of an expanding London. Although the area is covered by Green Belt the District Council still fear an invasion of Londoners.

Source: East Hertfordshire District Council, 1980.

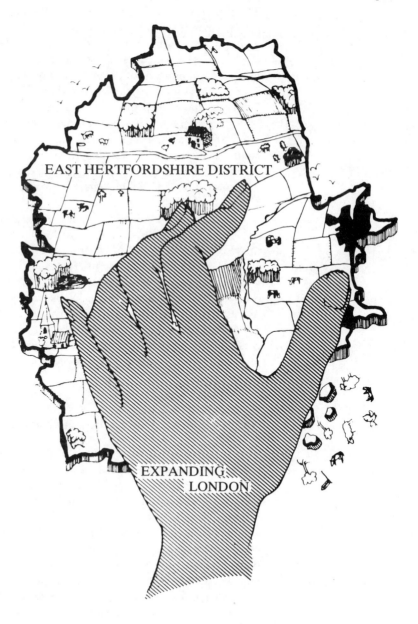

EAST HERTFORDSHIRE DISTRICT

EXPANDING LONDON

Wanting to stop change is a selfish though understandable attitude. In her book *New Lives, New Landscapes*, Nan Fairbrother (1970) has coined the expression 'shunters' to describe the way in which the effect of successful protest is to move urban development somewhere else and onto somebody else. It might seem that everyone is a shunter at heart but some groups welcome urban development, for example the unemployed, for whom the prospect of new industry represents a job; or small retail enterprises who see in redevelopment the possibilities of improved income from an influx of population in an area, or local authorities who might increase their rate income from new factories.

(c) Planners

Unlike developers and pressure groups, planners have nothing to gain personally from either development or protection of the environment. Their interest in land arises from the general goals of the planning system, namely the management of land in the interests of the community at large, including developers and the public. The planners' job is to regulate the activities of developers in accordance with the geographical patterns of development proposed in policies or plans. The planner's job is to identify areas and sites for particular kinds of land-use. Planners would claim that most of their work involves balancing conflicting interests in the development and protection of land. This balancing act is easier said than done. Planners must respond to prevailing political priorities: today (1989) the Thatcher government requires a non-interventionist approach to development pressures and controls cannot be applied rigidly in favour of environmental interests, a point taken up in Chapter 5.

The relationship between planners and politicians is not straightforward. Civil servants have considerable autonomy in handling the planning carried out by central government although they are accountable to Members of Parliament. The autonomy of local government planning officers is limited from two directions: by the policy of civil servants at higher levels and by the values of elected local representatives (e.g. County and District councillors) who have the final say on most planning issues. Party politics may affect how planning conflicts are resolved on a local scale, especially when decisions are taken 'en bloc' in council meetings or committees. Councillors may also act independently of party policy.

A simple model of the political environment

The simple model shown in Fig. 3.4 suggests how the four groups of players interact one with each other. National and local planning decision-making occupies the centre of the diagram, on either side of which are the decisions made by developers and environmental pressure groups. Much public input is 'reactive', only arising after a projected change has been proposed. The developer–local planning relationship is characterised by negotiation, lobbying and bargaining. When the planners make proposals they will have consulted developers and they will also seek to allay possible public fears about the impact of development by explaining the proposals at public meetings. Lobbying of elected members by the public may follow after planners or

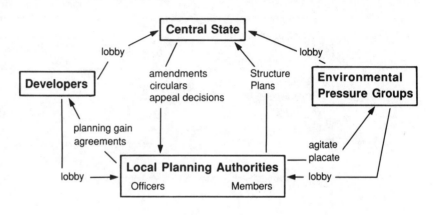

Fig. 3.4 Simple model of the political environment. Planning raises many conflicts of interest – the diagram suggests the channels along which these are resolved, via a combination of formal consultation and informal lobbying, bargaining and negotiation.

Source: Short, J.R., Fleming, S., Witt, S., 1986, *Housebuilding, Planning and Community Action*, London, Routledge and Kegan Paul, p.36.

developers have made their plans public. Both developers and environmental pressure groups lobby central government.

The model shows the direction of interaction between the key players. The decision process is seen to be rather messy, with local planners being pressed on all sides to react to the pressures of different groups. However, the model says nothing about the strength of influence each player brings to bear on the other. To help understand this, some case studies of conflict are helpful.

Conflicts

Many conflicts over the use of land become a battle between the interests of developers and environmentalists, with the planners stuck in the middle trying to resolve the differences between them. Of course this is not true of all conflict: the planners may be as opposed to development as are the environmental pressure groups, or vice versa. The arguments reflect a more fundamental difference of opinion about how best to control urban change; some developers may question the need for any government control and feel frustrated by what they see as bureaucratic meddling, while local people may feel their views have been squeezed out by the planners and developers.

Conflicts about the future use of land have their origins in aspatial conditions (see Fig. 3.5). There are worse hazards today than in the past, e.g. radioactivity and toxic waste. New lifestyles and social expectations have prompted the growth of environmental pressure groups who wish to resist urban change. Similarly, private sector pressures for land development are a response to changing market conditions and political encouragement. The different values held by each interest group are another source of conflict. Most major planning battles involve the question of whether economic values should override social and environmental values. In the case of large-scale infrastructure projects (e.g. new motorways or airports) it is usually central government that sets the condition for this conflict, by seeking to promote the national interest in investment and jobs.

Conflict is played out in the political environment. By looking at some case studies it is possible to analyse the different values and roles of each player in the conflict. Who stands to win and who to lose in the game? Which players appear to have most influence on the final outcome?

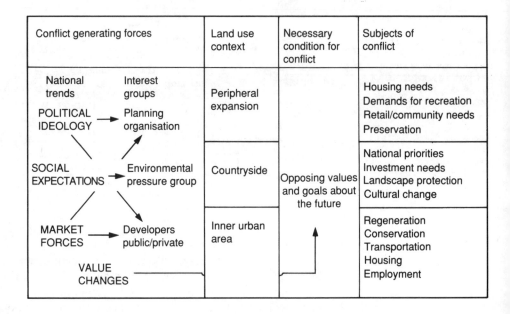

Conflict generating forces		Land use context	Necessary condition for conflict	Subjects of conflict
National trends POLITICAL IDEOLOGY SOCIAL EXPECTATIONS MARKET FORCES	Interest groups Planning organisation Environmental pressure group Developers public/private	Peripheral expansion	Opposing values and goals about the future	Housing needs Demands for recreation Retail/community needs Preservation
		Countryside		National priorities Investment needs Landscape protection Cultural change
VALUE CHANGES		Inner urban area		Regeneration Conservation Transportation Housing Employment

Fig. 3.5 A schema for studying locational conflict. The way different interests perceive the value of location is crucial to an understanding of planning conflict. Conflict will occur if there are opposing values and goals about the future. Some groups treat the environment as a resource to conserve for future generations, while others may see the opportunity for short term exploitation.

Source: constructed from Janelle, D. and Millward, H., 1976, 'Locational conflict patterns and urban ecological structure', *Tijdschrift voor Economische en Sociale Geografie* 67, pp. 102–113, Fig. 1.

Case study 1: conflict in the inner city

The causes of urban decay are the subject of widespread academic and public debate. Changing economic conditions have been crucial factors in bringing about the death of the manufacturing base, as Hoare (1983, p. 115) shows. The movement of population and employment out of the inner cities appears to be a long-standing and inevitable trend which governments may be powerless to reverse (Hall, 1985). Of importance too have been the planning policies of post-war governments which, by encouraging redevelopment, overspill and the creation of dispersed new communities, have contributed to a process of urban decentralisation to the outer city regions (Herington, 1984). While the arguments about the causes of inner city problems go on, the Thatcher government (1987) has made the regeneration of the inner cities a top political priority. Their solution to the problem of economic decline is to encourage a free enterprise spirit in the inner cities which will create investment and generate employment. Ironically, making this objective work has required considerable state intervention.

London's dockland

London's dockland (Fig. 3.6) is an inner city area which has suffered severe social, employment and environmental problems following the progressive closure of the East India, London and St. Katharine and Surrey Commercial docks between 1967 and 1970 and the West India, Millwall Docks and Royal Docks in the 1980s. In 1971, Peter Walker, then the Environment Secretary, announced in Parliament that an urgent study of the potential for rebuilding Docklands would be carried out. The local government organisations, the five London borough councils, together with the newly elected Labour Greater London Council, rejected the study when it was published on the grounds that it did not consider the ordinary needs of the local population for jobs and housing. In doing so they triggered off a series of conflicts between national and local government and between developers, environmental

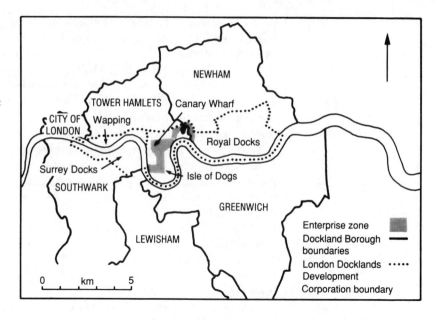

Fig. 3.6 London's docklands, showing the extent of land owned by the LDDC, the Enterprise Zone and Canary Wharf.

Source: adapted from Page, S., 1987, 'The London's docklands: redevelopment schemes in the 1980s', *Geography*, vol. 72, Pt.1., no. 314, January.

and community groups which have since characterised the politics of urban development in the Docklands.

A major source of these conflicts has been the free-enterprise philosophy of urban regeneration and the increased central government intervention which has been used to facilitate private sector investment. Local planners and politicians have emphasised the importance of encouraging change which will benefit the local community. They regard government policies as interventionist and undemocratic. The result has been an ideological battleground between the conflicting goals of wealth-creation and social welfare. Private development interests have effectively lobbied on a national scale while local councillors have sought to represent the views of local residents.

The conflict between central and local government is illustrated by the history of events between 1976 and 1986. In 1976 a new 'compromise' study was carried out by a partnership of local and central government planners who published the 'London Docklands Strategic Plan'. The plan showed in some detail substantial areas of proposed new housing in the Isle of Dogs and Newham, the proposed building of the Jubilee underground line, an extension of the London underground network east of Tower Bridge and new road bridges over the River Thames. The plan had some local political support but parliament and the civil servants failed to provide sufficient public resources to finance it. Despite the 1974 Labour government's introduction of a 'partnership' committee between central government, the then GLC and the Docklands' borough councils, to be responsible for programming the proposals in the plan, many projects were not completed mainly because they relied on major public expenditure. The incoming Conservative government of 1979 saw an opportunity for speeding up planning decision-making in the Docklands and created, after a period of intense political resistance from the local councils, private developers and residents' groups, a public development agency called the London Docklands Development Corporation (LDDC), the boundaries of which are shown on Fig. 3.6. This was rather like a New Town Corporation for the inner cities and it had wide ranging powers for the purchase of land, the provision of infrastructure, factories and houses, but it was not obliged to consult the public when preparing a development plan for Docklands, which had been the normal procedure in the New Towns. John Hall, a lecturer in geography at Queen Mary College, London, who has carried out extensive research into dockland issues, commented that the local boroughs and Labour parliamentary opposition saw the LDDC as 'extra-territorial political dictatorship, unresponsive to local desires and conditions'.

Since the establishment of the Urban Development Corporation for Docklands other Conservative policies for economic regeneration and planning have made their impact on the urban environment. With the tight limitation on public finance available, much encouragement has been given by the LDDC and central government to selling off land in the hope of attracting private investors. Those areas close to the City of London may prosper first, leading to a ripple effect eastwards. St Katharine's Dock has been substantially redeveloped for tourism and housing, while further east in the Isle of Dogs new private housing is under construction, although house prices are far too high for local people. More projects are being sponsored by private finance, for instance the Docklands Light Railway and the City Airport for short take-off and landing aircraft (STOL) located on the site of the Royal Docks. At the same time the government has designated part of the Isle of Dogs an Enterprise Zone (shown in Fig. 3.6), the purpose of which is to free developers from the possible restrictions of the planning controls which normally apply under the Town and Country Planning Acts (see Chapter 4).

A planning conflict between developers, the local community and environmental pressure groups has been generated by the proposal to build a £1.5 billion scheme at Canary Wharf, part of which lies within the Isle of Dogs Enterprize Zone. Developers, a consortium of Swiss and American financial and development institutions, have obtained approval from the LDDC for the construction of nearly 900 000 square metres of offices, hotels and shops in three skyscrapers 250 metres high, which would be the tallest buildings in Europe.

Developers argue that a project of this scale will have enormous benefits for the failing economies of Docklands: it will provide over 40 000 jobs directly and there will be a spin-off of new employment in secondary services such as offices, shopping and restaurants. The prospect of so many jobs would seem attractive to the thousands of unemployed in the East End of London, but the jobs will mainly go to skilled workers in the expanding financial services sector rather than to the predominantly unskilled or semi-skilled local residents. A political judgement is needed as to whether the economic benefits of the scheme outweigh the environmental and social costs. Developers clearly think that they will; the LDDC appears to be sympathetic to the developers, despite the view expressed by the Town and Country Planning Association that it is being hypnotised by a grandiose scheme which could easily become a white elephant. Several national and local conservation and amenity groups have voiced their fears about the excessive height of some of the buildings which would dwarf the architecture of Wren, Vanbrugh, Hawksmoor and Inigo Jones in the Royal Naval College and National Maritime Museum, described by the Royal Fine Arts Commission as 'the finest group of buildings in Britain'

Labels on image: PROPOSED CANARY WHARF SCHEME · ROYAL NAVAL COLLEGE · QUEEN'S HOUSE · NATIONAL MARITIME MUSEUM

Fig. 3.7 The possible impact of the Canary Wharf scheme on the London skyline. *Source:* Times Newspapers Ltd.

(see Fig. 3.7). Some amendments have now been made to the proposals in response to some of the objections raised.

The only other players who might have been expected to have a bearing on the conflict, the local planners, have been excluded from the decision-making process by the Enterprise Zone status, which meant that the developers did not need to obtain planning permission from the local authority, in this case the Borough of Tower Hamlets. Despite this, opponents of the proposal lobbied the Secretary of State for the environment to 'call-in' the development and to hold a public inquiry. This request was refused, on the grounds that the special status of the area would make it illogical for the State to intervene.

Some lessons

The developers and their financiers, supported by central government, appear to have won more influence over decision-making in docklands than either local government or the local community. In the Canary Wharf case the local planners were unable to control change in the urban environment since their planning powers had been effectively removed by Parliament. Nor were local people effective participants in the decision process. Negotiation took place between private developers and the London Docklands Development Corporation, a public agency set up by central government.

One important lesson from this study is the way in which a development project of this dimension has been decided without a publicly agreed planning and development strategy for the area. The Town and Country Planning Association argue that the social costs of the project have not been taken into account in decision-making: local people will gain little from the scheme except possibly from an increase in service jobs; there will be insufficient housing for workers in the locality of Canary Wharf thus extending commuting to areas where house prices are already escalating for other reasons, such as the

43

'Channel Tunnel effect' in Kent and the 'Stansted Airport effect' in Essex. The TCPA make a case for more positive strategic planning both on a regional scale and in Docklands, so as to avoid future 'ad hoc' decisions of the Canary Wharf kind.

Case study 2: conflict in the urban–rural fringe

Development pressures are intense on the periphery of cities because land is more plentiful and cheaper to develop than inner city locations. Because unplanned urban development may lead to unattractive urban sprawl, which is a wasteful and expensive use of land, planners have sought to protect the countryside from haphazard development by zoning land-uses for particular activities – housing, industry, open space and recreation and guiding future urban expansion in the form of compact clusters. Planned development in the urban–rural fringe would seem a sensible compromise between the need to find sufficient housing land for those living in the cities and the public's wish to see the countryside protected. Yet this kind of planning policy may still arouse fierce controversy as this case study shows.

Plans for the Leicester city region

The planning proposals for Greater Leicester were set out in the Leicestershire Structure Plan which was approved in 1976. It was one of the first Structure Plans to recognise the limitations of existing local government boundaries as a basis for comprehensive land-use planning. The area covered by the plan transcends the boundary of the City of Leicester and the pre-1974 Urban Districts of Oadby and Wigston and takes in 67 Parishes in the commuting hinterland, treating the whole area as one functional unit for planning purposes (Fig. 3.8). The planning sub-region covers about 52 000 hectares of which over 18 per cent are in some form of urban land-use.

The size of the future planning problem in Greater Leicester was simply stated in the Structure Plan. Policies were needed to deal with an expected population growth of about 122 000 and an employment growth of about 58 000 jobs over the 20 year period from 1971 to 1991. To meet this population growth and changing household characteristics, about 47 000 additional houses were required over the whole planning period. Housing and employment required about 2400 hectares of land for future development. With new and improved roads, additional schools and other forms of urban development, a total land take of about 2750 hectares was expected. The County and District planning authorities, Leicestershire County Council and Leicester City Council, had to produce a strategy to show where growth should occur and where it should not. The final preferred choice, seen in Fig. 3.8, sought to consolidate future urban growth in the urban–rural fringe around Leicester.

The aim was to produce a strategy which integrated housing, employment and transport requirements in the most efficient way. The distribution of industrial sites would be phased with housing areas to minimise growth of journeys to work into the city from the rest of the sub-region. However, the policy to a large extent reflected the spatial pattern of previous urban trends and sought to build upon them. Expansion would be channelled to places on the periphery of the city, particularly at Hamilton which would receive 19 500 people or 16 per cent of the expected population growth in Central Leicestershire. Other urban development was to be steered to selected large villages further out in the countryside. The arguments in favour of peripheral growth were as follows:

(a) it avoided longer distance overspill of population into attractive villages and thus protected the open countryside beyond the urban–rural fringe;

(b) by favouring a clear distinction between planned suburban developments and limited village growth, the strategy claimed to offer freedom of choice within the housing market for people who wanted to live in different kinds of environment;

(c) development close to the city could make use of existing investment in public utilities, schools and roads, thus leading to economies of scale which would not occur with dispersed urban development.

Unlike those of other major urban areas, the plans for the Leicester city region have never favoured the conventional use of a Green Belt beyond the outer boundary of the built-up edge of the city, nor have they included policies for overspill to New Towns. Rehousing has been directed to the suburbs close to the city boundaries and it is interesting to speculate where such growth might have occurred in the outer city region, had a Green Belt been defined.

Fig. 3.8 The Hamilton problem: the interests involved in the expansion of Leicester. Hamilton was to be a planned peripheral settlement of 19 500 population in the Structure Plan for Leicestershire, approved 1976. The original boundaries of the plan area overlapped the political territories of two District Councils. The main opposition came from residents living in small villages north of the defined site.

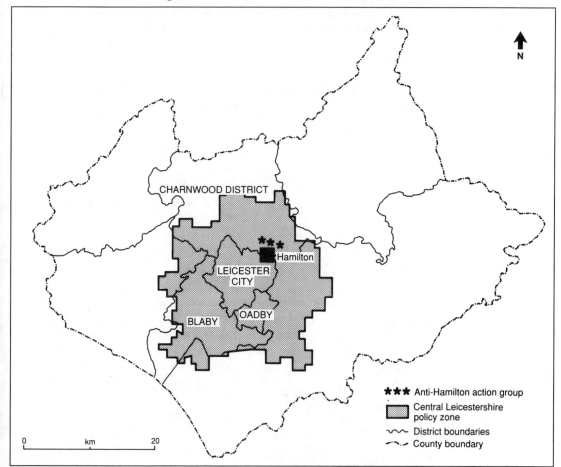

Problems of the Hamilton development

The area to be called the Hamilton development included three small villages and open farmland (Fig. 3.8). There was little public opposition to Hamilton when the policies were first being discussed at the time of the preparation of the Structure Plan. Unfortunately for Leicestershire County Council, the Structure Plan had already been approved before public protest made itself felt. The main opposition came when the scale of future urban development was indicated on the Local Plan. The 'stoppers' group composed of farmers and commuters came from the three small villages closest to, though not within, the designated area. They questioned whether it was desirable to divert new urban development onto greenfield sites (previously undeveloped land outside towns and cities) at a time of public expenditure cuts and the government's 1977 inner city initiatives. The planners argued that there was insufficient land in inner Leicester to meet the projected rate of household formation in Central Leicestershire and likely future migration. 'Stoppers' assumed that because population growth had slowed down at this time no new households were being formed and there was no case for further housebuilding. They also objected to the loss of farmland. 'Halt Hamilton, not harvests' was their emotive plea.

Following the publication of the Hamilton Local Plan the 'stoppers' successfully lobbied their District and County Councillors against the proposal. It was not until January 1983 that the County planners could obtain approval for a revised scaled-down plan, six years after the decision to delay work on the plan. The story was by no means over in 1984. Further public objections followed and the County Council was forced to reconsider the rationale for the entire project as part of the total strategy for the city region (see Table 3.2).

Table 3.2 Hamilton – anatomy of a conflict.

1976	Leicestershire Structure Plan approved by the Secretary of State. Hamilton Local Plan published.
1977	Opposition from local Conservative politicians leads to abandonment of Hamilton Local Plan.
1982	County Council elections leave no party with overall control.
1983	Leicestershire County Council Environment Committee approve revised scaled-down Hamilton Plan.
	Public Local Inquiry (PLI) at which many objections heard.
1984	Inspector recommends County Council should withdraw Local Plan for a total review of the case for Hamilton.
1985	County planners confirm need for Hamilton because of the deficiencies in housing land 1981–1996, but scale down proposals further from 4750 to 4200 dwellings.
	Revised Local Plan leads to further objections, but the County does not consider further inquiry necessary.
1985–6	County planners review the 1976 approved Leicestershire Structure Plan and confirm the importance of Hamilton Structure Plan. Examination in Public (EIP).
1986	Results of the EIP expected – will Hamilton be built?
1987	Secretary of State's decision on the modified Structure Plan gives the go-ahead for 4200 dwellings at Hamilton.

Ironically, by this stage in the decision process some of the major housebuilding companies were beginning to lose interest in Hamilton as a place to build. The market was changing: people preferred to live in smaller communities on small estates rather than in large new suburbs. It made more sense to disperse development more widely into the smaller villages beyond the urban–rural fringe. Strategic allocations on the scale of Hamilton were unnecessary because more houses were being built on sites which were not allocated on the Structure Plan, as a result of permission being granted to developers by central government on appeal (mentioned in Chapter 2). The County planners argued that there were no really satisfactory alternatives to Hamilton other than progressive urbanisation of villages, which would breach the principle of large scale consolidation in the urban–rural fringe.

After all this time the original Structure Plan needed review. Should Hamilton be abandoned as a major component of the plan? The County Council thought not, reaffirming its role as a major development area in the 'roll forward' of the plan. Yet another revised Local Plan was put before the public in 1985; there were still more objections, some to the principle and some to the details proposed in the plan. Some county councillors wanted to defer a final decision on the Local Plan until the 'Examination in Public' of the Structure Plan held in November 1986. Some wanted the total number of houses reduced to 2000. The story was still incomplete in 1986. The news of the Secretary of State's decision on the Structure Plan alterations did not come until 1987: only then was Hamilton confirmed.

Fig. 3.9 Expansion on the urban fringe. The first phase of three- and four-bedroomed detached housing development at Hamilton follows the completion of water and sewerage supply and the laying out of roads. Will residents of tower blocks in inner Leicester move out to Hamilton?

The lessons

The Hamilton saga demonstrates the important influence pressure groups have upon planning decisions. Hamilton was crucial to the success of the Structure Plan yet the development could not be started at the time it was needed because of local opposition. However, the victory of the 'stoppers' was more illusory than real: they successfully

staved off development for a period of ten years before central government intervened to give the go-ahead. Furthermore, changing circumstances in the housing market, especially the demand for and supply of land for housebuilding, played their part in how planners and developers reacted to the conflict over time.

Hamilton also highlights the weakness of a two-stage process of public participation in strategic planning. Only when policies were shown on a detailed plan did major resistance emerge and the Structure Plan policies had already been approved. Despite protest, were the County planners right to propose future urban expansion on this scale in the urban–rural fringe? This is a difficult question to answer since it is not known what might have happened if smaller sites had been selected. It is possible that developers would have protested more strongly than environmentalists!

Case study 3: conflict in the countryside

In the late 1970s the Vale of Belvoir, in the East Midlands, achieved national recognition when it became the focus of a bitterly opposed coalmining scheme. The conflict raised a national debate about whether the need for mineral exploitation should outweigh the need to protect the environment. The interests of government and the National Coal Board (now named British Coal) in productive investment and employment, came into direct conflict with the values of those wanting to protect the countryside, in particular landowners, farmers and an alliance of local residents and parish councillors. The scale of the proposed mining and its location in a hitherto protected and unspoilt area challenged local government countryside policies at County and District levels.

The Board submitted an outline planning application in 1978. Their intention was to mine 7.2m tons of coal per annum from three mining sites at Hose, Saltby and Asfordby in north east Leicestershire (see Fig. 3.10). They hoped to recover 510m tons out of a total reserve then estimated to be about 1300m tons at a total cost of about £800m.

Fig. 3.10 Location of three proposed coalmines in north east Leicestershire. Asfordby Mine was under construction in 1988. Note the intended use of disused railway lines for transporting the coal to the Trent Valley power stations.

Source: British Coal

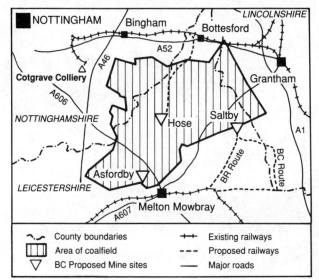

Although the proposals were often referred to by the media as the Belvoir coal mines, only one of the proposed sites, Hose, was actually in the Vale of Belvoir (Herington and Hamley, 1978). Because of the magnitude of the proposal the Secretary of State for the Environment 'called-in' the planning application (see Chapter 2). The arguments on both sides were then heard at a public inquiry which lasted 83 days; two years later, in March 1982, the Secretary of State for the Environment made a final decision. Speaking at the inquiry, Sir Frank Layfield QC, said, 'no single case since the end of the Second World War has been the subject of a planning inquiry where the proposals in question have had so great an impact on the English countryside . . . nor have any been promoted which are likely to continue over a greater period.'

The issues

The issues debated ranged from the need and cost of the coal to the effects on the landscape and community. They included:

1 National energy requirements, future consumption patterns and alternative sources of power;
2 The national need for coal and the cost of home production compared to imported coal. The benefits of leaving coal unmined for as long as possible;
3 Alternative locations for new coalfields and the justification for the three proposed sites; the life of other mines and the cost of Belvoir compared to alternatives;
4 The nature and amount of colliery spoil expected and the comparative costs/benefits of spoil disposal. The feasibility of remote tipping was also an important issue;
5 The impact of mining on agricultural land in the short and long term, including the prospects for effective restoration;
6 The visual impact of mine buildings and tipping and the possibility of reducing these impacts;
7 The impact of employment patterns on the local labour market, especially the indirect stimulus given to the creation of non-mining jobs; the impact of jobs lost as a result of the exhaustion of mines in Derbyshire, Leicestershire and Nottinghamshire;
8 The impact of employment growth on population growth; the effect of future migration on the numbers of houses and their spatial distribution. The need for and cost of additional public services such as education and social services;
9 The impact of a new population on the social character of existing village communities and towns.

Two issues in particular were at the heart of the conflict. Firstly, the Board's judgement that the coal would be needed. Leicestershire County Council, the strategic planning authority, with the environmental interest groups, challenged the economic case for mining. The Department of Energy forecasts showed the demand for coal for power stations peaking in 1990 at between 89m and 94m tonnes and falling to between 66m and 75m tonnes in the year 2000, suggesting that the Belvoir mines would come into operation just when a steep decline in coal demand was taking place. The Board argued that the costs of producing coal could be reduced by expanding production of new and cheaper coals from modernised pits; the strategy was to replace and in some cases supplement coal from high cost fields – a point which appealed to a government committed to improving the efficiency of the coal industry. Other new coal mining areas might follow north east Leicestershire, including Warwickshire, Oxfordshire, east Yorkshire and parts of Scotland. The inquiry inspector, Michael Mann QC, found it difficult to decide on the economic arguments for and against mining. Exactly when and how much coal would be needed in north east Leicestershire was impossible to say. Underpinning this discussion was the failure of the government to clarify national energy policy. The inspector thought that uncertainties in the government's nuclear programme might well reduce the future rate of decline in demand for coal for electricity generation.

The second big issue was whether, even if need could be proved, the Board had given sufficient weight to environmental objections. National and local issues were raised at the public inquiry. There would be important agricultural losses. Leicestershire's estimate for the loss in crop values was £20.6m over 50 years and £28.1m over 75 years, compared with the Board's figures of £3.2m and £4.9m respectively. The Board's estimated rate of tip restoration and the amount of land that would be out of use at any one time were questioned. Grave doubts were expressed by Leicestershire County Council about the scale of the visual impact of the mines and spoil heaps and about traffic, noise, and subsidence. The Board said that it was not opposed to finding alternative methods of waste disposal provided the government was prepared to finance these.

The environmental impacts varied somewhat in the case of each mine site as Fig. 3.11 shows. Undoubtedly Hose was the most politically contentious, particularly because of its impact on agricultural loss. The mine was to be the most productive of the three, producing 3m tons per annum, but nearly 50% would be spoil waste requiring 347 hectares of farmland to be taken out of productive use. This was likely to result in an estimated annual loss of £61000 in the gross value of agricultural production, although the Board pointed out that this figure would be less once the reinstatement of the land to agriculture had taken place in perhaps fifty years time. The National Farmers' Union voiced its opposition. The visual impact was also considerable and underestimated in the Board's environmental impact assessment (Fig. 3.11). The skip shaft at Hose was to be 58.3 metres, the equivalent

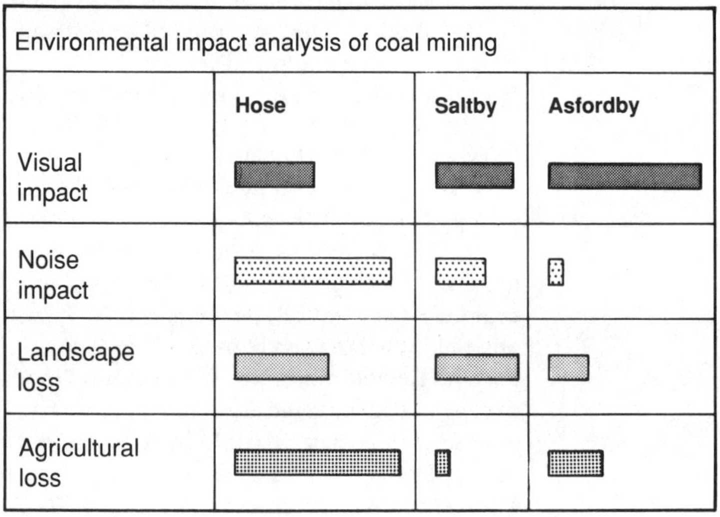

Fig. 3.11 Impressionistic bar chart showing the degree of impact of mining at each of British Coal's proposed sites. Each of four kinds of impact can be compared between sites (rows) but because each impact has been measured differently, different impacts cannot be contrasted for the same site (columns).

Source: adapted from Herington and Hamley, 1978.

Environmental impact analysis of coal mining			
	Hose	**Saltby**	**Asfordby**
Visual impact	▬	▬	▬▬
Noise impact	▭▭▭▭	▭	▫
Landscape loss	▬	▬	▭
Agricultural loss	▦▦▦▦	▫	▦

of a 17–19 storey building on the edge of the Harby Hills escarpment and thus clearly visible as far away as Nottingham. There was widespread opposition from local people and national environmental pressure groups, including the Council for the Protection of Rural England (see Fig. 3.12).

The Asfordby proposal raised the least environmental objection, partly because it was to be sited adjacent to an established industrial development, British Steel's Holwell ironworks, which had over 800 employees in 1977. The landscape impacts appeared to be much less than at the other two sites, but people living in Melton Mowbray would see the mine towers. There were social advantages in developing Asfordby which outweighed environmental considerations: the site was only 40 minutes from the north west Leicestershire coalfield where reserves would be exhausted by 1990. The demand for new housing and community facilities could be met within Melton Mowbray and Asfordby rather than by building in unspoilt villages.

Lessons

Despite the Board's insistence that coal mining was needed in the national interest, central government decided to reject the proposal on the grounds that mining would create unacceptable environmental costs. In refusing the planning application, Michael Heseltine, then Secretary of State for the Environment, overruled the recommendation of the inquiry inspector, Michael Mann QC, that permission should be granted, although spoil tips at Hose and Saltby should be refused.

Once again the power of environmental pressure groups in the planning process is illustrated by this conflict. The interaction between

Fig. 3.12 Protest in the Vale of Belvoir. *Source:* W. Hamley.

51

local government and environmental groups differed from Hamilton; at Belvoir the local planning organisations were as opposed to development as the environmentalists. However there are always winners and losers. The CPRE called the decision 'a major victory for good sense and rural England' while, in contrast, the National Union of Mineworkers reacted angrily and demanded early talks with the Board to avert rising unemployment among north west Leicestershire mineworkers.

Belvoir illustrates another feature of conflict: discordant values and policies within one level of planning decision-making. The Department of Energy was in favour of coalmining while the Department of the Environment was not. The final decision attempted to accommodate this national conflict of interest. The need to streamline the coal industry and take advantage of any potential job benefits were recognised in the DoE's decision letter to the Board. If the Board was to realise their mining objectives they would have to ensure their plans were not in conflict with environmental requirements. In effect this meant abandoning the Hose and Saltby sites which had proved most contentious. In autumn 1982 the Board duly applied for planning permission to mine coal at Asfordby. Permission was granted in 1983 subject to stringent conditions. By 1987 access roads had been constructed and the skip shaft, mine complex and tipping area were clearly visible.

Case study 4: inner versus outer city conflict

The expression the 'hole in the doughnut' has been used to describe the vacuum which developed in American towns and city centres in the 1960s and 1970s as households, jobs and retailers followed the freeways out of town, leaving the middle to rot. In Britain, dispersal of economic activity has been a major trend but planning controls have prevented it taking place on the American model. The perception of many planners is that market pressures could have grave social effects if the life is drawn out of established centres. The merits of permitting development outside town centres is also questionable when other aspects of economic policy are directed toward strengthening the cities.

One important factor in preventing large scale dispersal has been the large measure of agreement between government and retailers that shopping involving irregular purchases of goods (e.g. durable goods) should remain in town centres. The big out-of-town shopping centre has been seen as a cause, or at least a symptom of decay in the inner urban area. Until recently attempts to develop regional shopping centres on the edge of cities had failed, often after long running planning conflicts, for example Haydock Park in Merseyside in the early 1960s, Cribbs Causeway in Bristol, Stonebridge in the West Midlands Green Belt, Banstead Heights south of London and recently, Centre 21 near Leicester. There have been one or two notable exceptions, for example Carrefour near Southampton, usually granted on appeal by central government against the wishes of the local authorities.

In the 1970s supermarket companies turned their attention to suburban sites free from traffic congestion and with plenty of car-parking space. Local planning authorities relaxed their policy somewhat after initial opposition. One factor in this change of heart was the difficulty of balancing the need to conserve historic centres with provision for large new stores. Since then retailers have sought cheaper and more spacious decentralised locations for warehousing of bulky goods. However, in the 1980s there is a new pressure for what Schiller (1986) terms the third wave of retailing decentralisation to follow that of supermarkets and warehouses. This involves the dispersal of comparison shopping facilities e.g. a range of different clothing outlets in one centre, traditionally found only in city centres. It was signalled by the announcement in 1984 that Marks and Spencer was proposing to open out of town stores. These new shopping centres have a minimum floor area of 22 500 square metres and have been called regional shopping centres or 'megacentres'. Brent Cross in north London (Fig. 3.13), with 68 500 square metres could be described as a megacentre, but the most notable recent example is the 180 000 square metre MetroCentre in Gateshead's Enterprise Zone. The latest figures for September 1987 from Hillier Parker, a firm of chartered surveyors, show a total of 4m square metres of out-of-town shopping schemes, each in excess of 45 000 square metres, awaiting planning approval and a further 2m square metres for town centres. Applications have proliferated in central Scotland, around Leeds, Manchester, Birmingham and along the M25 around London, but they also affect Teeside, Southampton, Bristol and Exeter.

A new 'megacentre', which may combine comparison shopping with retail warehousing and other services such as fast-food restaurants, cinemas or banks, requires a substantial site with good road access, preferably near a motorway and a large catchment population. The building of a 'megacentre' could represent perhaps the greatest challenge yet to the survival of some traditional shopping centres and

Fig. 3.13 Out-of-town shopping: Brent Cross in North London.

Fig. 3.14 Out-town covered shopping megacentre – the £200 million retail, business and leisure development known as the Metrocentre includes major stores, a cinema and hotel, and may provide 6,000 new jobs in Gateshead Enterprise Zone. *Source:* Stewart Bonney (NEWS) Agency.

planning authorities are justifiably worried about their economic impact. The proposed scale of megacentres and their need to be located 'at the edge of the doughnut' also creates potentially major conflict with national and local planning policy because there are few urban-fringe sites which are not Green Belt. To get round these planning constraints retailers are looking to Enterprise Zones (see Chapter 4) although the larger developers are still pressing ahead with plans which involve taking Green Belt land.

Planners won many of the earlier battles over out-of-town sites and were supported by environmental pressure groups and central government. The issues are similar today: the threat to the cities, the threat to the countryside, the impetus given to other forms of decentralisation. But it is important to analyse the relative influence of retailers and planners in 1989 in the context of changing central government decision-making. Most of these new proposals seemed likely to fail but the fact that they exist perhaps reflects the more permissive planning regime under the 1989 Thatcher government.

Retailing pressures and the M25

One of the most important forces generating pressure for retailing development in the outer city has been the motorway building programme. By the early 1980s the Department of Transport was spending over £700m per annum on motorways and trunk roads in England. Some motorway links between major cities, for example, the M42 Birmingham-Nottingham link and the M40 London-Birmingham route, are still not completed.

The M25 London orbital motorway is 194 kilometres in length and encircles 8m people. It was built to strengthen the national and regional transport network and to provide industry and commerce with the benefits of higher productivity and reduced costs. Since it was completed developers have sought to exploit the improved patterns of accessibility which have brought centres like Guildford, Surrey, within 40 minutes drive of parts of Essex. Superstores, hypermarkets and retail warehouses were foreseen at the time of building the M25, but the much larger regional shopping centres were not. To date there have been nine proposals for regional shopping centres in the South East of which six are associated with the M25.

The existence of the M25 has enormously intensified speculation in land for retailing development and generated intense conflict of interest between local authorities, retailers and property developers. Fig. 3.15 shows the location of several proposed megacentres in relation to the Green Belt. The sites under greatest pressure are the key motorway interchanges, for instance, the triangle between the M1, M25 and A405, where Town and City Properties have applied for a 67 500 square metre shopping and leisure complex with 5500 ground level car parking spaces. Prudential Assurance, Britain's biggest institutional investor, has applied to Sevenoaks District Council for permission to build an 81 000 square metre shopping and recreational park at junction 4 of the M25, near Orpington. The developers hope to sell this project to the planners on the grounds that it maximises the recreational value of the Green Belt.

Local planning authorities have expressed their concern about the pressure for these very large shopping centres and their possible consequences. On the one hand they could foster economic growth and help revitalise the older urban areas – on the other hand their employment advantages have to be weighed against any detrimental effects on the countryside and on trading in existing centres. Conflicts have arisen on two scales:

A   National planning policy conflict   The motorway runs for its entire length through the London Green Belt which the government is committed to protect. 'The Green Belt is one type of area where,

Fig. 3.15 Development impact of the M25. Increased decentralisation of economic activity around London is one of the consequences of building the M25. Improved accessibility makes peripheral locations potentially profitable for commercial retail development; but 'megacentres' may conflict with Green Belt policy, threaten the viability of existing shopping centres and add to traffic congestion on the M25.

Source: adapted from Herington, 1984, *The Outer City*, London, Harper and Row, p.41. William Cochrane, *Financial Times*, October 18, 1986.

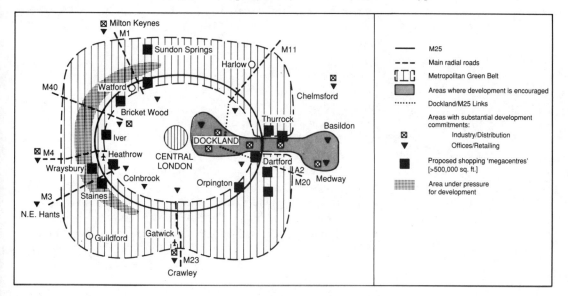

except for specially defined categories there is a presumption against development, be it a modest single detached house or a giant megacentre of 1 million square feet' said William Waldegrave in 1986 when he was Environment Minister. Ironically it was central government in the form of the Department of Transport that initiated the M25 and the Department of the Environment that was forced to produce new national policy guidelines on big shopping applications. In 1986 William Waldegrave announced that in future local planning authorities would have to consult the DoE before approving any development with over 22 500 square metres of retail floor space. In 1987 a draft circular to local authorities proposed that big shopping centres had no place in Green Belts nor were they acceptable in the open countryside; the only exceptions should be sites where derelict land could be reclaimed or when there would be a very diffuse impact on existing shopping centres. Lack of empirical evidence about the effect of out-of-town developments on city centres has helped to cloud this issue.

The new policy guidelines, if approved, appear to strengthen the hand of local authorities in resisting proposals for sites in the London Green Belt, unless they happen to be derelict. Counties and Districts may find it easiest to manage retail pressures in the southern and south eastern sections of the M25 because this is where Green Belt policy has been most effectively upheld by central government in the past. Retail pressures may be more difficult to resist in the eastern sector (shown in Fig. 3.15). In 1987 the DoE granted approval on appeal for a megacentre well in excess of 90 000 square metres sited in a disused chalk pit at Grays in Thurrock.

In another part of the guidelines the government seeks to weld shopping developments into its effort to promote urban regeneration by encouraging modernisation and refurbishment of town centres.

B   Intra-regional planning conflicts   The DoE's physical planning guidelines for the South East were set out in a brief statement in 1980: the aim was to increase the attraction of inner London for development, to maintain restraint in the Green Belt and provide for well-planned development beyond. Since then The London and South East Regional Planning Conference (SERPLAN) has produced new guidelines (1987) for shopping policy. These amount to a policy of:
1   doing nothing;
2   expanding or improving existing centres and not allowing any regional centres to develop;
3   permitting sufficient new centres to ensure all shoppers are within reasonable reach of at least one.

The existence of the M25 highlights the weakness of regional planning: the most attractive locations for developers to invest in have been created by central government itself precisely in the area of greatest planning restraint – the Green Belt. In addition, the stimulus to outer city growth occurs when inner London's economy is in trouble. A permissive attitude to retailing in the outer city would appear to conflict with both national and regional priorities for the regeneration of the inner cities, especially the London docklands. In theory the M25 has the potential for promoting the development of the London docklands, an area of employment decline, especially if transport links between the M25 and docklands are completed. However, a more likely scenario is that the motorway will act as a kind of self-fulfilling prophecy, shaping new patterns of accessibility and putting pressure on retail activity to move outwards at a faster rate than it can be attracted back to London. There will be nothing new about these events: by speeding up the dispersal of people and jobs, particularly along the motorway corridors north, west and south of London, the M25 will simply be reinforcing a process which was already under way.

The lessons

One interpretation of this study is that private developers have the initiative in the planning process. Decentralisation of retailing seems an inevitable trend while the planners must react in a passive way to the pressures being put on them. But there is a complex relationship between the perceived interests of the retailers and the role of planning decision-making at different levels. Central government also plays a leading role in the decision process through its direct initative in transport planning and development and its policing of Green Belt policy in conjunction with the local planning authorities. As development pressures have mounted, the government has been forced to step in with a form of 'crisis management' to give the Districts more power over the developers.

In contrast to Hamilton and Belvoir, the main players in this decision game have been the retail developers and the planners. There has been no direct role for environmental pressure groups to play, apart from their general support for the Green Belt concept. Planners at the local level, the Counties and Districts in the path of the M25, expressed their concern about the threat to the environment if the Green Belt were not held, but they were impotent to stop the motorway even if they had wanted to.

Summary

Political priorities play an important role in setting the framework for the four conflicts discussed in this chapter. Central government is a crucial player, directly promoting development, as in the M25 case, or working with the private sector, as in the docklands; sometimes it intervenes on the side of local government, as at Hamilton, or treads a tight-rope between environmental and production interests, as at Belvoir. The environmental lobbies appear at times to be on the winning side, delaying the time when building begins, or stopping change altogether, but their influence is often short lived. In many cases one level of planning decision-making is in conflict with another, or there will be conflicts within one level, as between different central government departments. Sometimes central government priorities will override local government planning altogether, as in the docklands example. In other cases, such as the M25, local planning organisations must live with major development projects and react to the development pressures which threaten to undermine their policies.

4 The effects of planning

Physical planning decisions have a long term, cumulative and direct influence on places and people. The nineteenth century industrial face of big cities has been transformed by the hidden hand of twentieth century planning: redeveloped neighbourhoods, new tower blocks, urban motorways and shopping centres are all familiar and sometimes socially disruptive elements of the urban scene. The impact of urban planning on the countryside has been no less pervasive: towns and villages have kept something of their physical identity, especially in Green Belts, while the influx of new populations into 'overspill' settlements has altered the demographic and social character of previously rural communities. Economic planning has also had far-reaching consequences: the provision of transport infrastructure, motorways and airports, the building of industrial estates and special financial measures have helped stimulate the development of some regions and restructure the economies of others.

The topics in this chapter are selected to enable a progressively broader examination of the effects of physical and economic planning on urban, settlement and economic patterns. Fig. 4.1 provides a conceptual framework based upon the idea of the functional region concept referred to in Chapter 1. The first two sections analyse the impact of various planning policies on urban and settlement geography using the terms defined in Fig. 4.1. The third section examines the role played by national economic planning in regional development.

Fig. 4.1 Observable effects of planning decisions on the regional city. Superimposed on geographical definitions of the city are selected examples of different kinds of planned change. The rural–urban fringe and rural hinterland around the central city provides space for new motorways which run through the Green Belt. The limits of the outer commuting zone are set by transport improvements in railway and road networks and the costs of journey to work. Public projects such as motorways, airports and New Towns stimulate the demand for private sector developments e.g. investment in housing, industry, commercial and retail enterprises, which in turn encourage population and employment decentralisation.

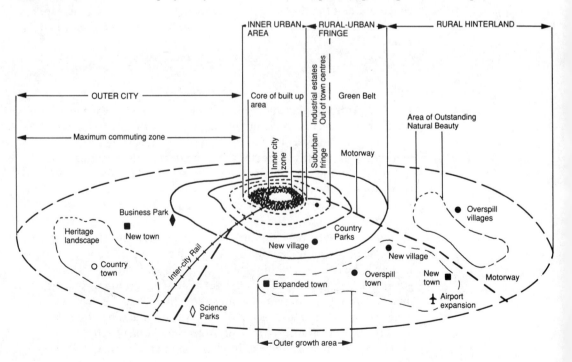

A Inner urban areas

The inner urban areas comprise the inner city and what are sometimes rather confusingly termed the outer city estates (which contain both local authority and owner-occupier housing). Fig. 4.2 defines these different kinds of areas in Liverpool. The inner city is subdivided by housing type and tenure into older terraced housing areas, rooming house areas and council estates. Within any city there are great contrasts in housing type, tenure and social status, as Fig. 4.2 shows for Liverpool. The social class composition of inner and outer council estates is unbalanced with a disproportionately high number of unskilled groups concentrated on the council estates.

The changing economic and social condition of the inner urban areas has presented government with a challenging set of planning problems. Different policies for dealing with the problem of urban transportation have been tried (e.g. urban motorways and improved public transport systems) often with mixed success; the problem of derelict and vacant land within inner cities has been tackled although far from resolved; redevelopment on a comprehensive scale has been used to tackle the apalling legacy of unfit housing and promote commercial office and retail development in city centres; on a smaller scale, area improvement has upgraded twilight zones of poor housing conditions; on the smallest scale, improvement grants have been made available to individuals and led to gentrification.

Urban planning codes and philosophies have had a significant effect upon morphology and social structure (see Fig. 1.6). Most of these effects have come about from the cumulative impact of government planning of various kinds at national and local levels. Evaluation of their effectiveness in resolving urban problems is always difficult. Ironically, what appeared once to be planning 'solutions' have now become problems – this was certainly true of the wholesale demolition and tower block fashion in the 1960s – and it may prove true of the

Fig. 4.2 Housing tenure and socio-economic status contrasted between the inner and outer estates of Liverpool. Residential segregation results from redevelopment and overspill within a context of national housing policy.

Source: Adapted from Department of Environment, 1977, *Change or decay. Final report of the Inner Area Study (Liverpool)*, DoE, HMSO

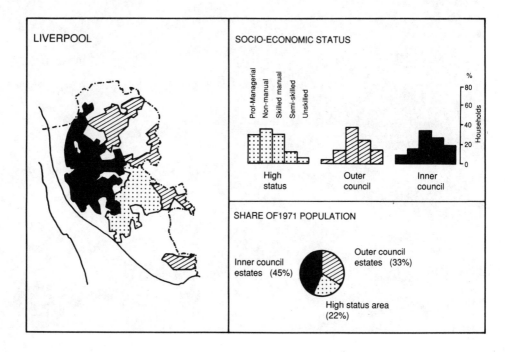

'enterprise culture' of the 1980s. Perhaps just because particular 'solutions' easily become fixed doctrine it is only later than their unintended consequences become evident, a point which applies to New Towns and Green Belts as well as to the inner cities.

Redevelopment

Of all urban planning policies, comprehensive redevelopment schemes have undoubtedly had the most dramatic impact on the physical and social geography of cities. The 1947 Town and Country Planning Act provided the basis for the designation of thousands of CDAs (Comprehensive Development Areas) in British cities. Very large areas of mid- or late Victorian age housing, industrial and commercial development were demolished in the inner areas, sometimes in conjunction with the building of new ring roads. Slum properties and old back-to-back housing were replaced by high and medium density housing in tower blocks.

A comprehensive approach to urban problems was understandable given the immediate post-war effects of bomb damage in major cities. Large scale slum clearance was a response to the deterioration in the condition of inner area housing, the overcrowding of households and the acute shortage of housing. The scale of the problem is well illustrated by Glasgow (Fig. 4.3). Studies in the older districts of Glasgow such as the Gorbals revealed densities as high as 160–200 persons net per hectare at a time when the Ministry of Town and Country Planning was recommending no more than 50 persons per hectare net. The case for large scale redevelopment was reinforced by

Fig. 4.3 The slum problem was acute in the Gorbals district of Glasgow. The ground floor of these flats was still inhabited in the mid-1950s. *Source:* BBC Hulton Picture Library.

the publication of the 1951 Census which for the first time enabled a comparison to be made between the degree of overcrowding in the seven conurbations of Great Britain. Over 43% of the Clydeside conurbation was found to be living at residential densities in excess of 1.5 persons per room. Densities had to be lowered and rehousing of the population either on the periphery or outside the city became imperative. Moreover, the population of the cities was not static – new households were being formed, thus adding to the total number requiring alternative accommodation following redevelopment. By the mid-1940s it was estimated that 550 000 people, half the then population of Glasgow, would need to be displaced from redevelopment areas if redevelopment were to take place. The Glasgow experience was replicated in many other British cities, although not on such a dramatic scale.

With time, redevelopment was seen to have several important social consequences. Firstly, it led to segregation of different types of housing tenure across the city. The 1960s attempts to tackle the problem of obsolescent housing produced many large local authority built housing estates in the inner and outer areas while the intermediate areas remained substantially in privately owned or rented accommodation (see Fig. 4.2). The shortage of land within cities for new private owner-occupier housebuilding drove the movement of new families into suburbs, while increasingly the remaining population in the inner city became characterised by the less mobile, poor and elderly. It is important to remember, as Sims' (1984) research has shown, that the problems of deprivation and stress in the inner city are found also on outer local authority housing estates. Deprivation may be attributed in part to the political history of comprehensive clearance and the mass provision of one class housing. While this argument oversimplifies a complex issue, it is true that extensive reliance on uniform public rented housing areas has widened the social differences between rich and poor and led to dramatic concentrations of deprivation in cities such as Liverpool.

Secondly, there was the effect upon population redistribution and internal migration within cities. Newly cleared sites could never rehouse the same number of people because higher standards of housing and improved layouts needed more space. The problem was aggravated when most new building took the form of houses rather than tower blocks of flats. Thus the critical questions for planners were: at what density should population be rehoused? Where could the people be rehoused? The scale of the land deficiency problem varied considerably. Many city authorities had to hunt for land outside their administrative boundaries or seek boundary extensions which enabled them to provide the necessary housing. Other cities were able to contain the rehousing of population within their boundaries.

Geographical analysis of the pattern of residential and social mobility reveals that within the public housing sector, local authority boundaries effectively created sealed migration systems. Outward moves from the redeveloped inner city were largely to peripheral local authority housing estates, because of the system of council housing allocations which accompanied the rehousing programmes. Moves in the private sector, which were not directly influenced by redevelopment schemes, were also peripheral in character, often to the suburbs and villages beyond the city boundary, because this was where the new private housing was being built. Both kinds of movement were interrelated: large-scale redevelopment 'pushed' people outwards while private sector housebuilding and public sector overspill schemes 'pulled' them into the suburbs and beyond. Both processes led to a shift in the population from the inner to the outer city. However, studies of housing mobility in Glasgow carried out during the 1980s suggest a significant change in the pattern of residential mobility which is linked to recent policies for regenerating the city. Private housebuilders have begun to favour sites in the inner city ('brownfield' or redevelopment sites) in preference to greenfield sites, thus encouraging an in-movement of some private sector households. There also appears to be a drift back from the worst of the outer public estates by those able to buy themselves back into areas of good housing repair.

Thirdly, there have been the destructive social effects of comprehensive redevelopment. Social and structural deficiencies in some of the 'high-rise' and 'deck-access' housing have gradually become apparent and today present severe problems for local housing authorities. In her book *Utopia on Trial* (1985) the geographer Alice Coleman has drawn attention to the possible connection between high-rise development and the incidence of crime and vandalism (Fig. 4.4). Other social problems have been noted: the alienation of families and broken kinship networks are serious enough, although they have their comic side (Fig. 4.5); employers lose their workers as the density of population falls, existing workplaces disappear as industrial premises are cleared. Perhaps one of the best known studies of the socially disruptive effects of post-war inner area urban renewal and overspill was written by the sociologists Young and Willmott. Their book, *Family and Kinship in East London* (1965) records the fragmentation in family and kinship relationships in Bethnal Green as the population is rehoused on a new estate some distance away. 'When the town planners have set themselves to create communities anew as well as homes, they have still put their faith in buildings . . . But there is surely more to a community than that.'

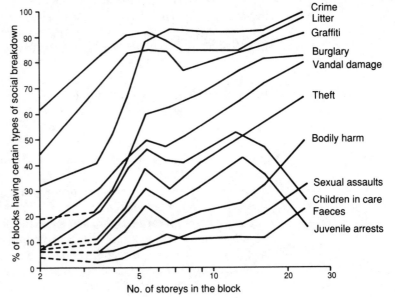

Fig. 4.4 Social breakdown and height of tower block. The crime curves mostly show a break of slope at the threshold level of three storeys and thereafter rise more steeply. Families with children are regarded as not at risk in walk-up blocks without lifts and in the lowest four or five floors in high-rise buildings. But do tall buildings cause crime?

Source: Coleman A., 1987, 'The social consequences of housing design' in Robson, B., *Managing the City*, London, Croom Helm, p.147.

Fig. 4.5 Satirical comment on the social effects of high-rise housing redevelopment. The break-up of family networks was seen as the result of insensitive urban planning.

Source: *Punch*, McCrae, Cartoon

"Wave bye bye to Gran!"

Case study: St. Ann's, Nottingham

The consequences of redevelopment may be examined in space and over time. The example of St. Ann's, one of the most recently redeveloped areas of slum housing in Britain, suggests that it is dangerous to generalise about the social failure of redevelopment. St. Ann's was an area built in the late nineteenth century for Nottingham's industrial working-class. By the 1960s it was a neglected and congested area of 10 000 Victorian houses in various stages of decay and collapse. Jumbled among the houses were factories, shops, pubs, churches, small workshops and corner shops. Demolition seemed inevitable because the houses were in such poor structural condition and lacked basic amenities – 91% had outdoor lavatories only and 85% lacked bathrooms. Diseases closely related to poverty were widespread e.g. bronchitis, arthritis, rheumatism. There were no green areas, modern schools or community facilities.

The whole of St. Ann's was bulldozed and replaced by new housing at a lower density (Fig. 4.6). Between the late 1960s and mid-1970s a large estate of 3500 new council houses was built on the cleared land. At the beginning of redevelopment the population of St. Ann's was approximately 30 000. Only about 35% of the original 10 000 dwellings were replaced in the scheme i.e. 3500 and the population in the new St. Ann's was approximately 10 500 (1969 figure). The result was a substantial forced movement of 19 500 persons (65% of the old

Fig. 4.6 The low-rise two- and three-storey redevelopment of St. Ann's Nottingham, showing construction in progress during the early 1970s. *Source:* Evening Post, Nottingham.

St. Ann's population) mainly, though not exclusively, to other large Nottingham Corporation housing estates around the western perimeter of the city (Fig. 4.7). Indeed only about a quarter of the original inhabitants were able to return to the new St. Ann's. Apart from the overspill factor, the mechanism of council housing allocation used by local authorities resulted in some of the new houses being allocated to families in need from the general housing waiting list, thus further reducing the opportunity for former St. Ann's residents to return to the area they had once lived in.

A number of good points emerge from this example, some of which are not typical of redevelopment schemes. Some overspill families were clearly glad to move out whatever the disruption to their way of life; others appeared not to mind to which area of the city they had to move provided they had a better property, while those who were owner occupiers in St. Ann's resented having to move in the first place and having to become tenants of rented property. However, most households reacted favourably to the move, settling in happily and expressing satisfaction with the new environment.

In spatial planning terms St. Ann's was an exceptional redevelopment scheme in the sense that two- and three-storey houses and flats, built in terraces, were preferred to tower blocks. The physical condition and appearance of the area was greatly improved. As the plan shows, houses are arranged in a more open, spacious and less congested road pattern, with gardens and courtyards and busy through traffic routes being separated from pedestrian ways (see Fig. 4.7). Much satisfaction has been expressed with the quality of the housing in the new St. Ann's compared to the old. However, there are some bad points. The variety of small workshops and pubs has gone and with it the opportunity for local work, particularly for part-time employment. Accessibility to shops has worsened with fewer shops at a greater distance – the old St. Ann's contained a variety of specialist traders, butchers, grocers and second-hand shops: today there is only a small shopping precinct with a

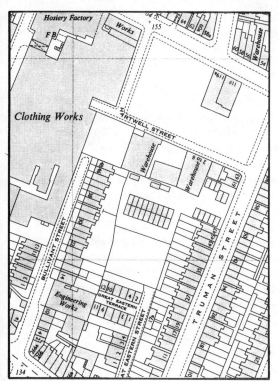

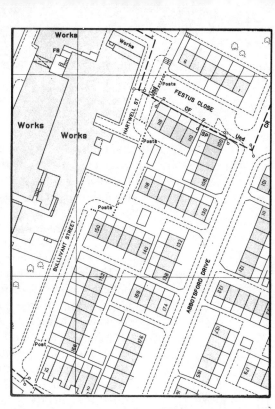

Fig. 4.7 Redevelopment and overspill estates in Nottingham 1919–83. Part of St. Ann's before and after redevelopment in the 1970s. Substandard dwellings were demolished and replaced by housing at a lower density. The local engineering works was removed to make space for the housing. People were found new homes on peripheral council estates.

Sources: Brown, P.A., 1984, 'The development of Nottingham', in Brazier, S., Hammond, R. and Waterman, S.R., *A New Geography of Nottingham*, Nottingham, Trent Polytechnic, p.35. Gillespie, J., 1975, *'Residential mobility and preference in the St. Ann's district of Nottingham'*, Nottingham University Department of Geography (B.A. Dissertation).

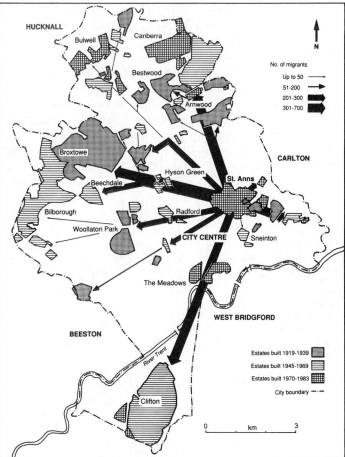

65

small general store. Antagonism and suspicion between neighbours has replaced the familiarity and supportive social network found in the old slum environment; crime and vandalism have increased.

Area improvement

Since the early 1970s there has been a reaction against the comprehensive schemes of the kind employed in St. Ann's, partly on economic and social grounds and partly through a desire to retain as much of the infrastructure as possible. Other housing policies took over from slum clearance, as seen in Fig. 4.8. The latest phase of local authority housing and planning policy has concentrated on more gradual improvement rather than wholesale clearance of substandard dwellings. In practice, clearance continues in most cities today where pockets of unfit housing remain, although on a greatly reduced scale.

Housing and area improvement became a major element of urban policy after the 1969 Housing Act introduced the concept of the General Improvement Area (GIA). The legislation also allowed for individuals to receive grants to renovate their properties. The 1974 Housing Act added the concept of the Housing Action Area (HAA) to apply to remaining areas of greatest housing stress, often areas which physically lay between redevelopment areas and GIAs.

Progress on area improvement has had a gradual impact on inner cities, bringing the local planning authority into a more interventionist role in relation to a larger and larger proportion of the city's housing stock. Birmingham presents a classic example of the extensive nature of these new policies, which have been added to the earlier and continuing phase of redevelopment and reflected in the spatial structure of the city. A 1981 report estimated that the City Council's urban renewal programme consisted of 110 existing or proposed GIAs containing 55 617 properties, plus 46 HAAs containing 18 584 properties. However, even these figures look small against the estimated further 70 000 properties requiring substantial investment to prevent them falling into decay. The policy of improvement, as with redevelopment, depends essentially on financial resources being available from within the public and private sectors. One advantage of improvement is that it

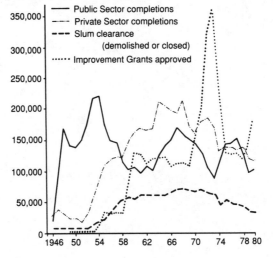

Fig. 4.8 Housing policy outputs 1946–80. Reaction against wholesale slum clearance and changing political priorities saw the dramatic rise of housing improvement during the early 1970s. Improvement is still favoured in the 1980s because it is cheaper and less damaging to established urban communities.

Source: Short, J.R., 1984.

delays the much more substantial cost of redevelopment for perhaps 15–20 years on the life of an individual property. However, if funds are insufficient to carry out improvement comprehensively and within a relatively short time scale, the problem of dilapidation increases, ultimately requiring the clearance of dwellings which become unfit to live in. Thus in the long term the problem of inner city decay is unlikely to ever be solved entirely by a policy of improvement.

Gentrification

Area improvement has had its greatest impact on the zones lying between the central business districts and the suburbs, the so-called twilight zones of cities and towns. Although the visual impact has been less striking than clearance and redevelopment, the improvement policy has affected the physical structure and functioning of local residential areas as well as encouraging gentrification. Gentrification is the process whereby lower income tenants and owner occupiers have been replaced by newer, more affluent groups.

Case studies in different British cities have shown that the policy of giving improvement grants has tended to favour mainly owner-occupiers in 'decent working class' areas rather than people in private rented or twilight areas suffering the worst housing conditions. In some parts of inner London the grants allowed landlords to upgrade their properties and sell them to private households wanting to move back from more distant commuting areas – the effect was to displace working-class tenants and fuel a buoyant property market. This process has continued in particular areas of London and is now associated with the in-migration of 'Yuppies' (Young Upwardly Mobile Professionals) who are prepared to pay exorbitant house prices for a home in the city near to a highly-paid job (Fig. 4.9).

Summary

Important questions for society are raised by the experience of redevelopment in cities, especially in the context of the social unrest that occurred in places like Brixton, Toxteth and Handsworth during the 1980s. Were municipal authorities right to knock down and rebuild inner areas on this scale? Were they sufficiently sensitive to the needs of the resident populations? Could some of today's social problems have been avoided by the more cautious policy of housing improvement rather than by wholesale clearance and rebuilding? At the heart of these questions is a difficult debate about the extent to which planners may be held responsible for worsening social conditions in the cities, particularly lack of employment. It was naive of the architects and planners in the 1950s and 1960s to believe that by making changes to the physical environment within which communities live, people's life-styles and behaviour patterns would also be transformed. On the other hand, we cannot ignore the fact that redevelopment has helped improve the personal and living environment of many people. Unfortunately there have been wider consequences for society. Planners have done their best to encourage people to move out from the cities into new communities but many of the elderly, young and ethnic groups have

Fig. 4.9 'Yuppie' housing in London's Docklands – part new build, part conversion (of Victorian soap factory) for luxury housing, Bridewell Place, Wapping. *Source*: Barratt East London Ltd/DCN.

been left behind in this process. Some would argue that this trend is both inevitable and desirable – the aim of planning policy should be to reduce the population density of the inner cities further and encourage people to find jobs and homes elsewhere. Yet just as redevelopment and clearance have had important effects on the inner city, so a policy of urban decentralisation will have consequences for the outer city – a theme we turn to next.

B   Outer city settlements and countryside

In the aftermath of World War II, Britain's planners set about reconstructing the conurbations and encouraging the decentralisation of population and industry. A process of widespread new urbanisation was begun, stimulated in large measure by the need to decentralise from London and the major conurbations and by the perceived need for the construction of motorways. This process transformed the form and functions of many settlements in the countryside around the conurbations, creating a new kind of post-industrial regional city (see Fig. 4.1). Over time, greater personal mobility, especially the greater use of the car for journeys to work, has extended the functional boundaries of regional cities over the greater part of lowland Britain. Areas falling within the main commuting hinterland of the city, notably the outer parts of the regional city, have witnessed particularly dramatic rates of population growth and accompanying decentralisation of employment (Tables 4.1, 4.2 and 4.3).

Table 4.1 Flight from the cities. Highest rates of percentage population decline, 1971–81, are found in the largest cities while the fastest rates of growth occur in the surrounding countryside, especially the planned growth towns.

	Decline	Growth	
London	−9.9		
Other conurbations	−4.6		
Other large cities	−5.1		
Smaller cities	−3.2		
Industrial towns		+3.0	
		+4.9	Resorts and retirement areas
		+7.0	Partly rural areas
		+10.3	Rural areas
		+15.1	New Towns

Source: adapted from Census of Population, 1981

Table 4.2 Manufacturing change by type of sub-region, 1959 – 75. An urban – rural shift in employment performance is suggested, with the largest percentage increases being in semi-rural and rural areas.

Type of subregion	% of total UK manufacturing employment, 1959	Change 1959–75	
		'000s	%
London	18.4	−585.9	−37.8
Conurbations	32.5	−433.7	−15.9
Major free-standing cities	21.8	+61.6	+3.4
Smaller free-standing cities	4.3	+64.0	+17.9
Industrial non-city	18.7	+254.8	+16.3
Urban non-industrial	1.3	+41.7	+38.8
Semi-rural	2.1	+78.2	+44.9
Rural	1.1	+73.1	+77.2

Source: based on Fothergill and Gudgin, 1979, Table 3.2.

Table 4.3 Employment change in the South East, 1971–81 (1968 Standard Industrial Classification). The decline of manufacturing has been less and the growth of services more rapid in the suburban and rural areas outside London (ROSE = Rest of the South East counties).

	Manufacturing	Services	Total
Inner London	−186,722(−40.6)	−105,041(−6.1)	−318,300(−13.9)
Outer London	−192,047(−32.6)	+98,681(+10.2)	−95,622(−5.8)
OMA	−125,370(−18.4)	+237,233(+25.0)	+111,604(+6.3)
OSE	−15,337(−3.5)	+231,111(+23.9)	+210.487(+13.6)
South East	−519,476(−23.9)	+461,984(+10.0)	−91.871(−1.3)
GB	−1,963,200(−24.9)	+1,703,000(+14.5)	−501,200(−2.3)
Berks, Bucks	−11,106(−3.0)	+208,190(+32.1)	+196,595(+17.6)
Other ROSE counties	−129,601(−17.2)	+260,154(+20.5)	+125,496(+5.7)

Source: SERPLAN, 1984

69

These are the patterns we observe today. How did planning influence them? To answer this it is necessary to return to another basic question being asked nearly half a century ago: can society control the physical growth of big cities? The problem of very rapid urban growth was particularly great in the inter-war period in Britain. The social and environmental disadvantages of allowing big cities to expand too rapidly, particularly London, were highlighted in the historic Royal Commission report on the distribution of the industrial population in England and Wales (Barlow Report, 1940). This report recommended that the way to avoid congestion was for governments to impose strict control over the spread of housing and industrial development on the fringes of major cities and to disperse people and jobs to emptier regions which would welcome additional development. This solution to the problem of urban growth was called urban containment; the principles of containment became enshrined in the post-war planning legislation.

Although the term is used somewhat confusingly in the literature, many commentators agree that urban containment comprises two related planning objectives: the physical protection of the countryside and planned urban development. Containment is associated with two very important planning concepts: firstly, the Green Belt and secondly, the creation of planned new communities. The negative powers of development control in the 1947 Town and Country Planning Act provided the bricks upon which to build the protective arm of urban containment. The concept of Green Belts was devised in part to stop the outward physical spread of cities into the countryside, thus reinforcing the impact of the planning Acts. Where the Green Belts were drawn around existing settlements, as in the case of some of the London County Council out-county estates built in the 1930s, some population growth was inevitable within the Green Belt (Fig. 4.10). But

Fig. 4.10 Inter-war and early post-war estates and New Towns in the London region. The relative absence of overspill schemes south of the River Thames in London was due in part to local political opposition.

Source: Blowers, A., 1973, 'Planning residential areas', in *Planning and the City*, The Open University: a second-level course in urban development, DT 201 27–29, p.106.

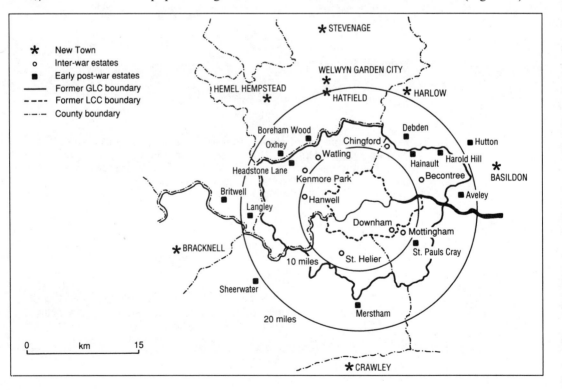

Fig. 4.11 Greater London Plan.

Source: Cherry, G.E., 1981, *Pioneers in British Town Planning*, London, Architectural Press Limited.

Fig. 4.12 Sir Patrick Abercrombie, author of the Greater London Plan, 1944. This was possibly one of the most influential regional plans in Britain, since so many of the proposals were implemented. The concept of Green Belts and planned New Towns was applied to other big cities in the post-war period. *Source*: Godfrey New Photographics.

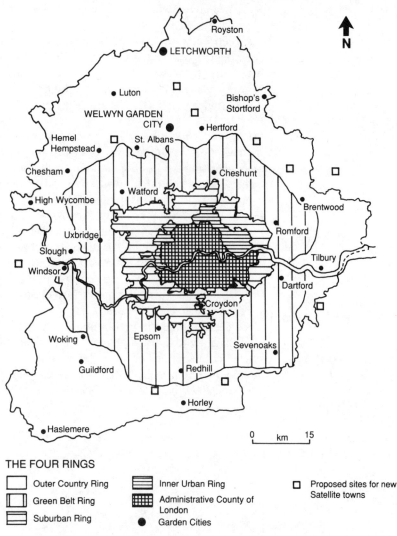

THE FOUR RINGS

- ☐ Outer Country Ring
- ☐ Green Belt Ring
- ☰ Suburban Ring
- ☰ Inner Urban Ring
- ▦ Administrative County of London
- ● Garden Cities
- ☐ Proposed sites for new Satellite towns

it was intended that the general policy of restraint could only be breached when new urban development took the form of planned new communities.

No standard model of planned settlement was suggested by Barlow, rather a combination of overspill estates, new suburbs, garden cities and the creation of New Towns and the expansion of existing ones well away from the conurbations (Figs. 4.11 and 4.12).

When analysing the effects of containment the geographer needs to remember that the related policies of countryside protection and population dispersal have been applied in rather different forms at different times, depending on the city–regional context.

Effects of containment policy

1   Green Belts   The purposes of Green Belts were summarised by the Ministry of Housing and Local Government in Circular 42/55: Green Belts should prevent urban sprawl and the coalescence of settlements and protect historic towns from fringe development. Land within the Green Belt would remain for the distant future in agriculture or recreational use while most forms of urban development would be directed elsewhere.

Green Belts were not approved until the mid-1960s around Birmingham and later still in West Yorkshire and Tyne and Wear. It is often forgotten that not all cities have statutorily approved Green Belts. Mention was made of Leicester in the previous chapter. Cardiff, Hull and Norwich may be added to the list of cities without Green Belts (see Fig. 4.13).

(a) Restriction of growth – London, Glasgow, West Midlands   How and with what effect Green Belt policy was put into practice can be judged by contrasting the London and Glasgow Green Belts. In both cases, the Green Belt in conjunction with overspill policies has been a means of shaping rather different spatial patterns of urban growth. The London Green Belt was established by Act of Parliament in 1938 and used in planning control after Abercrombie's Greater London Plan (1944). The plan for a Green Belt in Glasgow was first proposed in The Clyde Valley Plan (1946) and not officially approved until 1951.

The London Metropolitan Green Belt was a device for stopping urban growth in particular areas. Urban development has been more severely restricted than in the Glasgow case. Over 75% of the London Green Belt remains in predominantly rural use – mainly farmland and woodland – with a small proportion, possibly 4–5% at most, in settlement use. Furthermore, the overall rate of land taken for development has been quite low: one estimate suggests that between 1963 and 1974 the extent of villages and small groups of houses may

Fig. 4.13 Statutorily approved Green Belts in England and Wales. 1986.

Source: Munton, R., 1986.

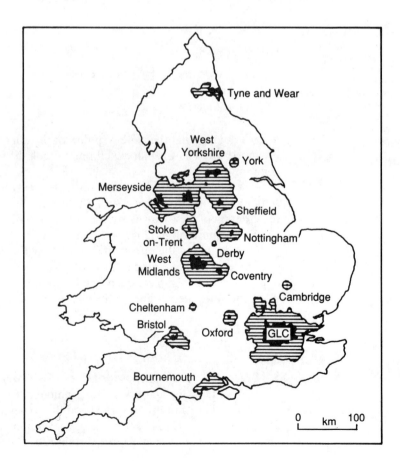

have risen by over 1000 hectares from a figure of 8000 hectares, or 3.5% of the total area of Green Belt in 1963 (Munton, 1983). However, even with this apparently rigid collar type of Green Belt, local planners have found it difficult to resist pressures for some urban development to the west and east of London (Fig. 4.14).

In contrast, the Clyde Valley Green Belt – in part because of the unique terrain and settlement distribution near Glasgow – took the form of a green sea within which was located an archipelago of urban areas, including Glasgow itself. One possible disadvantage of the Clyde Valley Plan was the likelihood that it would prove difficult to prevent the pressure building up for some urban development within the Green Belt setting (Fig. 4.15). However, much high quality agricultural and amenity land has been protected from urban development. Nor has Glasgow merged with the surrounding settlements to create the kind of continuous urban sprawl we associate with some American cities. In this sense the Green Belt has helped successfully to shape the form and pattern of settlement change close to the conurbation.

Fig. 4.14 Net increase in developed areas between 1947 and 1969 in the Green Belt as defined in 1975. Why do you think some local authorities found difficulty in resisting the pressures for development despite the existence of Green Belt?

Source: Munton, R., 1983, *London's Green Belt: Containment in Practice*, London, Allen and Unwin.

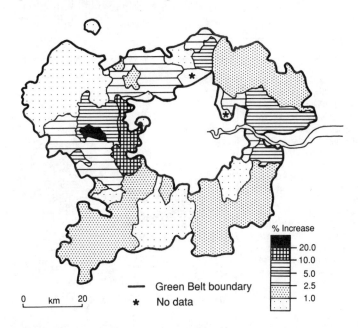

Some of the most dramatic spatial effects of Green Belt policy are discovered by plotting the distribution of planning refusals. If it is assumed that all refusals would have been approved, a pattern of the probable growth of settlements without Green Belt control is revealed. David Gregory's classic (1970) study, *Green Belts and Development Control*, demonstrated clearly for the area west of the West Midlands conurbation that the spread of the conurbation had been very effectively contained during the late 1950s and first half of the 1960s (Fig. 4.16). Gregory noted that the Green Belt was not powerful enough to restrict all development to the areas where it was planned. Moreover, the general effectiveness of Green Belt policy changed over time: it had proved more difficult for local planners to resist pressures for building in the first half of the 1960s compared to the late 1950s. This shows that were it not for the Green Belt, the countryside surrounding many cities and towns would be more developed than it is today.

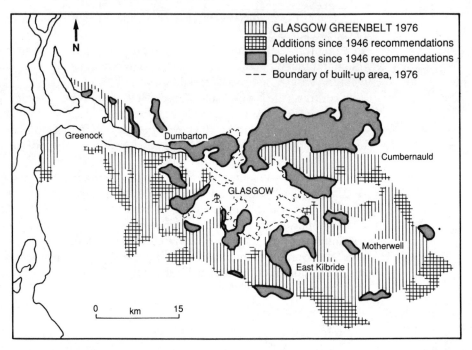

Fig. 4.15 Changes in the Glasgow Green Belt since the 1946 Clyde Valley Regional Plan. Considerable sections of the original Green Belt are not found in the 1976 plan, suggesting greater chance of future urban growth on the inner boundaries south of the city and beyond the outer boundaries to the north.

Source: Adapted from Smith, R. and Wannop, U., 1985, *Strategic Planning in Action: The impact of the Clyde Valley Regional Plan, 1946–1982*, Aldershot, Gower, p.50.

Fig. 4.16 Probable growth of the West Midlands conurbations without planning controls, 1957–66. Analysis of what would have happened in one District if planning refusals had been permitted. The conurbation would have spread dramatically, creating a continuous urban sprawl north/south and extending two miles west into the rural area.

Source: Gregory, D., 1970, *Green Belts and Development Control: A Case study in the West Midlands*, Centre for Urban and Regional Studies, University of Birmingham, Occasional Paper No. 12. p.30.

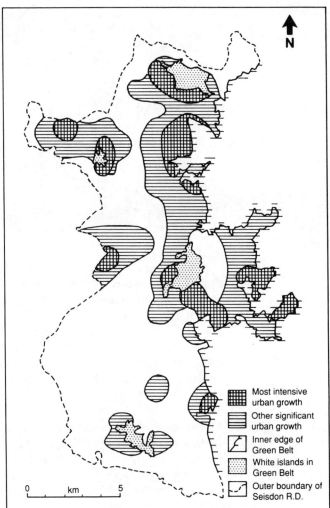

Fig. 4.17 Population of towns in Britain's outer cities 1971–81 in relation to Green Belts. In most metropolitan regions (see Fig. 1.7) population has spread out beyond the boundaries of the Green Belts, although in Merseyside and West Yorkshire a much greater degree of population growth has stayed within the Green Belts. Why should this be so?

Sources: adapted from Herington, 1984; Munton, R., 1986.

(b) Socio-demographic effects   As well as the perhaps obvious land-use impact of the Green Belt policy, there are other hidden socio-demographic side-effects. The restriction of housing land supply within settlements in Green Belts tends to inflate property values there, making it difficult for new households of local people to afford housing. Thus, small new private housing developments in these settlements tend to be occupied by families of high socio-economic status groups (see Table 4.7). Those low-income families needing to rent houses face a diminishing supply of Council dwellings or, if they wish to buy, they are forced to find houses in less expensive areas, either in suburban estates or in planned growth settlements beyond the Green Belt. Some lower paid, key service workers have become as Pahl (1975) described them 'reluctant commuters', who have moved out from the inner urban areas not because they wish to live in the countryside, but simply because they cannot afford a house in the city.

The demographic effects of Green Belts are hinted at by the spatial patterns of population change 1971–81 (Fig. 4.17). The wider areas

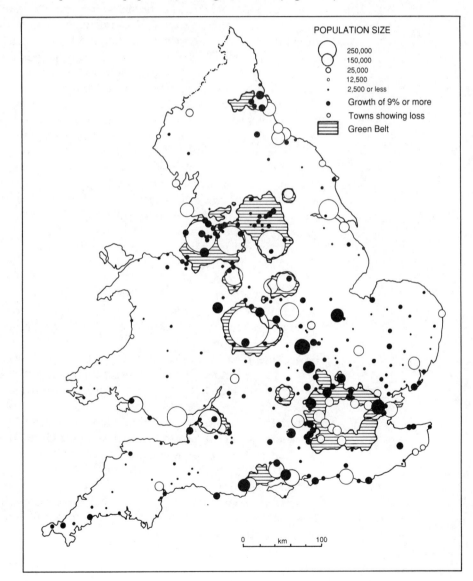

POPULATION SIZE

◯	250,000
◯	150,000
◦	25,000
∘	12,500
·	2,500 or less
●	Growth of 9% or more
○	Towns showing loss
▤	Green Belt

0   km   100

beyond the Green Belts have seen an increase in total population. Not all of this growth can be attributed to the direct influence of the restriction of growth within the Green Belts themselves. Mostly the influence has been indirect, deflecting housing pressures to smaller country towns and villages, thus helping to bring about a general and unintended dispersal of population growth within the city region. A 'knock on' effect of people moving further out has been the lengthening journey to work and consequent expansion of commuting hinterlands. What Green Belts have done is to increase the separation between homes and workplaces and thus add to the journey to work problem. These effects were seen most dramatically in the London region during the 1950s and 1960s before substantial decentralisation of jobs from London had got underway. Similar patterns are evident around other rapidly growing Green Belt cities, such as Bristol, Nottingham, Derby, Southampton–Portsmouth and Bournemouth–Poole.

(c) Economic effects   It is argued, though difficult to prove, that the economic impact of Green Belts has been to raise the value of urban land within the cities. Faced with having to house their populations within their own boundaries, the cities have been forced by expensive land prices to build high-rise housing. But despite rehousing programmes the cities have lost population through decentralisation of population; it could equally be argued that the economic effects of outward migration have helped to promote intensive housebuilding as much as high land values. Outward migration of the better-off has eroded the tax base of the city councils. At the same time the massive rehousing of the less well-off, encouraged by the housing subsidies offered to local authorities by central government, seems a logical way of retaining some income for the city. Because it has generally been owner-occupiers who have left the cities, most of this low-income housing has taken the form of subsidised municipal building. The causes and effects may be complex but the physical reality is seen in the social separation between public housing in the city and private housing in and beyond the Green Belts – an aspect touched on in the previous section.

(d) Political effects   Green Belts have had the unintended effect of heightening social and political polarisation between the inner and outer city. Outer city residents have grouped together to oppose what is seen as an invasion of townspeople, which would threaten their environment and lower property values. Green Belts have become a political battlefield as they come under threat for piecemeal development (Fig. 4.18). Many Conservative controlled local councils have successfully warded off development pressures and Labour dominated city councils have found themselves reluctant allies of the Conservatives in jumping to the defence of the Green Belts, partly to stem any further loss of population and rateable value from the inner cities. However, both Conservative and Labour politicians have been willing to sacrifice Green Belt principles for perceived national or regional economic necessities, as demonstrated by the building of the National Exhibition Centre in the West Midlands Green Belt, or Kodak in the Nottingham Green Belt.

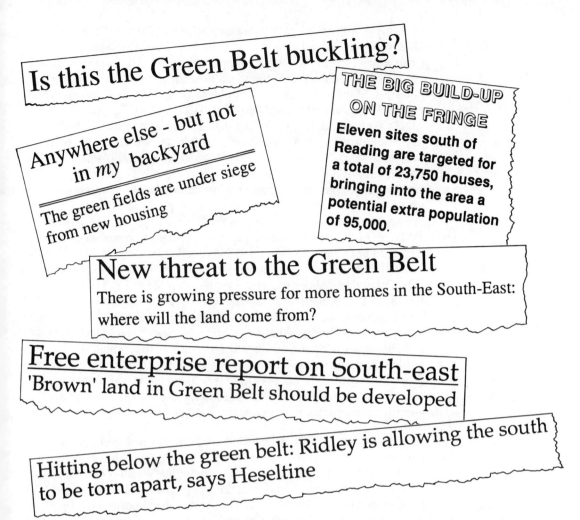

Is this the Green Belt buckling?

Anywhere else - but not in *my* backyard
The green fields are under siege from new housing

THE BIG BUILD-UP ON THE FRINGE
Eleven sites south of Reading are targeted for a total of 23,750 houses, bringing into the area a potential extra population of 95,000.

New threat to the Green Belt
There is growing pressure for more homes in the South-East: where will the land come from?

Free enterprise report on South-east
'Brown' land in Green Belt should be developed

Hitting below the green belt: Ridley is allowing the south to be torn apart, says Heseltine

Fig. 4.18 The political impact of the Green Belt is seen in the attention given to Green Belt issues by the media during 1988, much of it related to the London Metropolitan Green Belt.

2   New and Expanded Towns

The removal and redirection of people from cities has affected many types of settlement. Housing estates have been sited on the outer edges of city boundaries, there have been suburban expansions in the rural–urban fringe and growth in smaller rural settlements within the commuting hinterland. Planned dispersal to industrial and agricultural towns has taken place and even entirely new towns have been created on greenfield sites.

The scale, pattern and settlement form associated with planned dispersal varies greatly both between and within urban regions. Rehousing schemes have taken many forms, not necessarily involving recourse to the powers provided in the New Towns (NTs) and Expanded Towns (ETs) legislation; for example West Yorkshire, Bristol and Liverpool before 1961. There was an important difference between the NTs and ETs constructed under the 1946 New Towns Act and the 1952 Town Development Act. Designated NTs were built by a government-appointed Development Corporation which had the power to choose where to locate the NT, to acquire land, provide water, gas, electicity and other necessary services and carry out the necessary construction. In contrast, over 100 towns in Britain were expanded under the powers of the 1952 Town Development Act, through

77

agreement between an 'exporting authority' – usually, though not always, towns within a conurbation – and the 'receiving authority' – any town which took the initiative to import overspill. Thus London had agreements with thirty-two different local authorities, Birmingham had eighteen, Manchester and Liverpool four each, Newcastle-upon-Tyne two, Bristol four and Glasgow forty-two (Table 4.4).

NTs are commonly classified by date of designation and planned population size. Mark I NTs comprise the first fourteen that were built pre-1950, Mark II the period 1951–61 when only one NT was designated, Cumbernauld; and Mark III settlements cover the substantially larger NTs designated since 1961. Mark I and III towns differ in population size as well as urban morphology. However, there are significant variations in the regional location, population growth rates, socio-economic composition and economic performance of NTs which do not reflect this Mark I–III distinction (see Fig. 4.19).

The British NTs are praised abroad as one of the finest examples of urban planning and design. These virtues should not be understated, but the policy of planned decentralisation has had wide ranging social consequences, which are sometimes neglected by observers who focus solely on the architectural aspects. The scale and speed of urban change and the consequent distortions which occur in demographic and social structure are the main features of NTs and ETs. Other problems are essentially 'contrived' because they arise from the stated strategic goals of planners, namely to relieve congestion in the big cities and create socially balanced communities in terms of jobs and homes.

(a) Population   The 32 British NTs are home for just over 2 million people. By 1985 the combined population of the English NTs was 1 784 025, of the Scottish NTs 254 989 and of the Welsh NTs 55 600. Seven NTs in England had populations of over 100 000. The largest NT in Scotland is East Kilbride with a population just in excess of 70 000. The size of the Town Development Agreements varied greatly: some were very small, for example Kings Lynn, but others such as Basingstoke, Swindon and Tamworth were able to match the NTs for scale of both population and employment growth. Until the end of 1979 (when the statistics ceased to be gathered) the total population of the ETs of England and Scotland was about 305 000 – of which 55% were in the London schemes.

The demographic impact of the New and Expanded towns programme is evident at both national and regional scales. The 1981 Population Census reveals that, almost without exception, the fastest growing places in terms of both absolute percentage rates of change, have been the NTs and ETs in the outer cities (Table 4.5). But there are spatial variations in the rate of change. Away from the conurbations the population 'performance' of some towns has been disappointing, while giants like Milton Keynes and Peterborough have demonstrated phenomenal growth patterns (Fig. 4.19).

(b) Jobs   National policy for the location of industry has played a hand in determining the economic success or failure of New and Expanded Towns. Sadly, there was no co-ordination between regional location of industry policy and the planned programmes administered by the DoE. In many respects the DoE's policies for the Assisted Areas hindered the economic prospects of NTs and ETs located in non-Assisted Areas.

Table 4.4 Expanded Towns in England: public housing and factories completed under Town Development Act schemes.

	Dates of TDA Scheme	Dwellings Built	Factories No. of firms	Factories Floorspace m sq ft
Birmingham schemes				
Aldridge & Brownhills	1960–1974	938	30	0.3
Banbury	1961–1966	235	0	0
Cannock	c 1957–1980	638	10	0.2
Daventry	1963–1976	2,255	95	3.7
Droitwich	1964–1981	1,778	30	0.9
Lichfield	c 1957–1975	1,039	0	0
Rugely	c 1957–1971	130	10	0.2
Stafford	c 1955–1975	421	0	0
Tamworth	c 1959–1981	5,107	111	1.4
Tutbury	c 1957–1971	49	0	0
Uttoxeter	c 1955–1965	200	0	0
Weston Super Mare	c 1958–1972	802	12	0.4
Total		13,592		2987.1
Manchester schemes				
Burnley	1967–1974	14	0	0
Crewe	1965–1975	50	0	0
Macclesfield	1959–1968	750	29	0.8
Winsford	1959–1966	564	39	2.6
Total		1,378	68	3.4
Liverpool schemes				
Burnley	1967–1974	132	0	0
Ellesmere Port	c 1960–1974	2,413	0	0
Widnes	1964–1974	853	18	0.5
Winsford	1964–1972	2,627	57	2.9
Total		6,025	75	3.4
Wolverhampton schemes				
Cannock	1960–1973	343	0	0
Seisdon	1955–1964	1,546	0	0
Tettenhall[1]	c 1953–1966	131	0	0
Wednesfield[1]	c 1953–1966	2,450	11	0.7
Total		4,527	11	0.7
Newcastle upon Tyne schemes				
Cramlington	1963–1980	1,795	41	3.5
Killingworth	1962–1980	1,957	44	1.0
Total		3,752	85	4.4
Bristol schemes				
Keynsham	c 1955–1960	642	0	0
Sudbury	c 1955–1966	136	0	0
Thornbury	c 1955–1966	500	0	0
Warmley	c 1955–1961	1,000	0	0
Total		2,278	0	0
Salford scheme				
Worsley	c 1953–1966	4,518	0	0
Walsall schemes				
Aldridge	1954–1960	215	0	0
Brownhills	1954–1958	229	0	0
Total		444	0	0
Total all expanded towns		87,013	2,105	62.4

*There was also a TDA agreement between Birmingham and the town of Leek but no houses or factories were built.

1. The major part of these local authorities was amalgamated with Wolverhampton in 1966.

*The dates of some schemes cannot be precisely identified.

Source: *Town and Country Planning*, November, 1984

Table 4.5 Largest relative population changes 1971–81: towns with a 1981 population of 10 000 or more.

	Largest increases		
Town and county	*Status	1971–1981 population increase– percentage	1981 population
Washington (Tyne and Wear)	NT	102.6	53 783
Milton Keynes (Buckinghamshire)	NT	102.0	106 974
Runcorn (Cheshire)	NT	78.1	64 117
Redditch (Hereford and Worcester)	NT	63.1	66 854
Tamworth (Staffordshire	ET	59.6	64 315
Witham (Essex)	ET	46.0	25 373
Seaton Valley (Northumberland)	ET	44.1	46 141
Bracknell (Berkshire)	NT	43.1	48 752
Guisborough (Cleveland)	ET	42.8	19 903
Thetford (Norfolk)	ET	42.7	19 591
Skelmersdale and Holland (Lancs)	NT	42.1	43 464
Droitwich (Hereford and Worcester)	ET	41.8	18 073
St Neots (Cambridgeshire)	ET	39.3	21 185
Haverhill (Suffolk)	ET	38.0	17 146
Daventry (Northamptonshire)	ET	36.9	16 178

*NT = New Town, ET = Expanded town

Source: Herington, J. 1984, p.29

Fig. 4.19 Annual population growth rate of New Towns in Britain (excl. Northern Ireland). Average per annum growth rates have been calculated from the difference between the 1985 population of New Towns and their original population at time of designation, divided by the number of years since designation. The map thus reflects both variations in the age of New Towns and the size of their original population (60 in the case of Aycliffe, 82 500 in Milton Keynes). High rates of growth are not solely a function of population size: Glenrothes and Livingston grew by 37 000 in total since designation, but Livingston's annual growth rate was almost twice that of Glenrothes. Slowest rates of change were New Towns with particular economic prolems e.g. Corby, Central Lancashire.

Source: compiled from statistics in *Town and Country Planning*, 1986, vol. 54, no. 10, p.285.

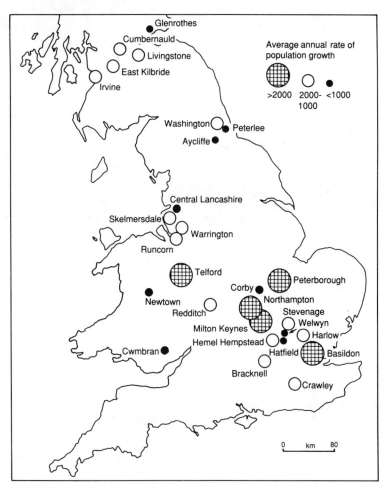

Under the Town and Country Planning Act 1947 a system of Industrial Development Certificates (IDCs) was set up for all new and extended factories above a certain threshold size. The threshold was raised to 4500 square metres in 1979 but during the time of planned decentralisation it had been 450 square metres. The DoE's regional policies gave priority to granting IDCs to manufacturing industry in the Assisted Areas rather than the NTs (and since 1978 the inner cities have taken priority over the Assisted Areas). The ETs received no special priority under regional policy. Nor have other decision-making agencies like the Council for Small Industries in Rural Areas (COSIRA) and the Development Commission, encouraged by central government support for small businesses, given any special priority to ETs over and above other small towns.

Changes in the level and structure of employment in NTs have occurred since their designation, although the data is difficult to obtain. There has been a 50% increase in the number of employed; though the share of manufacturing jobs has in general fallen while that of services has grown. The extent to which this increase represents a net gain to the country as a whole, as opposed to a transfer of jobs, remains a subject of contention.

Given the absence of government support it is perhaps not surprising that the NTs and ETs have attracted only a relatively small proportion of new manufacturing jobs. Nevertheless, relative economic 'boom' conditions have been obtained in some NTs in the South East – Milton Keynes, Northampton and Peterborough for instance – where locational advantages are strongest. Employment growth has been notably less dramatic in other NTs in north east England, possibly a reflection of wider regional economic decline. Some NT's in Assisted Areas have benefitted from regional policy, East Kilbride for instance. Merseyside's Special Development Area status may have had an effect on the high level of Regional Development Grant allocated to companies in Runcorn.

One of the main problems in NTs and ETs has been co-ordinating the creation of new jobs with the growth of population to ensure that there would not be a labour surplus. In the early London NTs, only those who had a job could move, but this requirement was later relaxed. Ironically, those NTs which have been successful in generating new jobs have experienced relatively high unemployment rates, simply because the population has grown faster and larger numbers of people are entering the labour market. Fig. 4.20 shows that NT unemployment rates are higher than surrounding Counties, but with the exception of Corby, none experience higher unemployment than is found in the inner cities.

(c) Social balance   The social class structure of planned towns contrasts with the inter-war unplanned housing estate. For example, Dagenham is largely one-class with the majority of the population in semi-skilled or unskilled occupations. In the 1960s the NTs were able to recruit a more socially balanced population than Dagenham, with significantly higher proportions of professional jobs. The mix of social groups living in any planned town depends partly on the employment and housing opportunities available. Heraud's (1968) classic study revealed the limited opportunity for unskilled and semi-skilled employment in the London NTs (Table 4.6). The effects of town expansion on social class

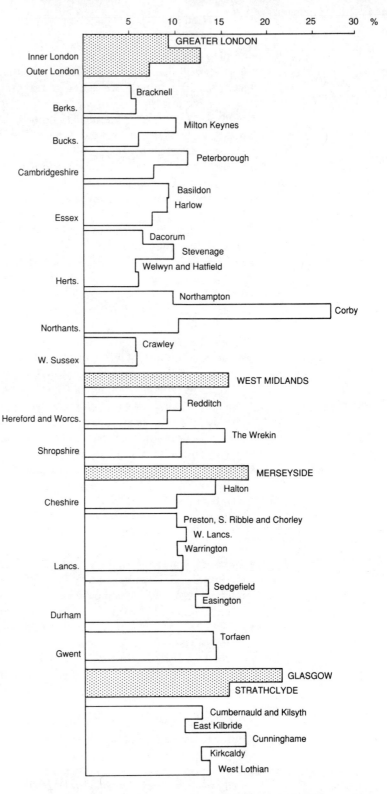

Fig. 4.20 Unemployment rates in Districts containing New Towns, nearby conurbations and surrounding Counties, 1981. Unemployment rates of the largest New Towns in the South East exceed that of Greater London but not that of Inner London. In most other regions unemployment is higher in the conurbations than in New Towns. Why have New Towns performed better do you think?

Source: Potter, S., 1982, 'Britain's New Towns: what the census shows', *Town and Country Planning*, vol. 51, no. 10, p. 282

and socio-economic structure are less well documented. However, Harloe's (1975) study of Swindon refers to the effect new firms had upon the migration of upper middle class groups and semi-skilled workers following town expansion.

New and Expanded Towns may be criticised for failing to meet the

Table 4.6 Class structure of London New Towns in the 1960s.

Social Class	Crawley 1961	Harlow 1957	Hemel Hempstead 1960	England and Wales 1961	Greater London 1961	Dagenham 1958
I Professional	3.7%	5.0%	5.9%	3.8%	4.8%	1%
II Intermediate Professional	13.4%	13.0%	20.1%	15.4%	15.8%	4%
III Unskilled non-manual and skilled manual	63.6%	63.0%	54.6%	51.1%	52.2%	56%
IV Semi-skilled manual	13.1% }	19.0%	14.4%	20.5%	18.1%	22%
V Unskilled manual	6.2% }		5.0%	9.2%	9.1%	17%
Middle Class (Classes I & II)	17.1%	18.0%	26.0%	19.2%	20.6%	5%
Working Class (Classes III, IV and V)	82.9%	82.0%	74.0%	80.8%	79.4%	95%

Source: Heraud, B.J., 1968, 'Social class and the New Towns', *Urban Studies,* vol. 5, no.1, February, pp.33–58.

real housing needs of the urban poor. In this they have probably failed, but it is questionable whether achieving a notional balance of social classes was ever a very realistic or desirable social objective. Changing housing policies in the NTs and ETs would seem to make equity goals even harder to achieve today. Recent sales of Development Corporation houses and the rising importance of shared ownership and privately owned houses, is encouraging the migration of the middle income skilled groups at the expense of the semi- and unskilled.

(d) Mobility and journey to work   Although a large number of migrants to the NTs and ETs came from the cities, over time the source of in-migration has changed as more people have moved from neighbouring regions and settlements. As a consequence the functional role of new settlements has changed from that of dependence upon the parent conurbation to one of interdependence within a wider network of settlements making up the outer city.

The changing function of NTs is reflected by new patterns of journey to work movement. At a time of low car ownership it was perhaps reasonable for planners to assume that every resident of a New Town should be able to find work locally without travelling to other areas. Today more than three-quarters of all households in NTs have at least one car. The functional relationship between NTs and the conurbations changes over time. Most overspill settlements undergo a similar cycle of change in their commuting patterns, as suggested in Fig. 4.21.

(e) Decentralisation and inner city decline   The New and Expanded Towns legislation was used to relieve congestion in the cities. During the 1960s the high rates of natural population increase, in-migration and declining household size contributed to the rapid rates of growth of some of them. In the 70s and 80s they have been blamed for the problems faced by the inner cities and the government has ended official decentralisation policy. However, as Champion's (1977) research shows, the planned schemes need putting in perspective: they represent only a small part of a far more general process of decentralisation which causes concern to the cities. It would be misleading to say that the NTs and ETs played a major role in the

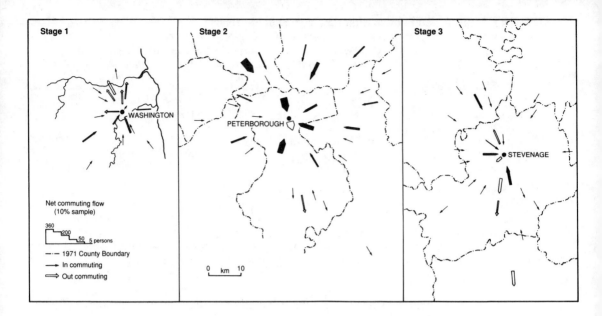

Fig. 4.21 The cycle of change in New Town commuting patterns. Three stages are identified. Stage 1 – population growth exceeds employment growth with a resulting excess of outward commuting journeys, usually back to the conurbation. Stage 2 – the growth of local jobs reduces out-commuting; some New Towns prove very successful in attracting more jobs than are available to local residents, with the result that people commute in from surrounding areas. Stage 3 – other housing and labour markets compete with the New Town, resulting in out-migration and out-commuting. The final stage sees complex functional linkages emerge between the NT and neighbouring settlements within the outer city.

Source: derived from Champion, A.G., Clegg, K., Davies, R.L., 1977

population loss from the inner urban areas, although their influence varies over space and time. In Scotland about 65 000 people left Glasgow over the period 1966–71 under the official overspill programmes, about 30% of the total net exodus. In England there was a marked contrast between Liverpool and London. In the former, overspill accounted for 10–15% of all out-migration. In the case of the London region the NTs and ETs programme took a much smaller proportion of all out-migration from the capital.

3 Commuter settlements

Although the physical expansion of settlements in rural areas other than New and Expanded Towns has not been controlled by legislation or agreement, it has nevertheless been subject to control by local planning authorities and subject to scrutiny by central government. This kind of planning is often referred to as rural settlement planning. It lacks the degree of commitment to low-cost housing or the provision of balanced employment and social facilities that we associated with the NTs and ETs. Nonetheless a distinction has been drawn between 'key' and 'non-key' settlements (see Fig. 4.23 for a definition) in Structure Plans covering parts of the outer city, and this policy has had an important relationship to the wider dispersal process in the outer city (Fig. 4.22).

The selection of higher order or 'key' settlements is based on a range of variables: for instance, population size, transport services, numbers of schools, shops and other community facilities in relation to population. New housing and community services are provided in existing larger villages rather than being dispersed to many villages, in order to protect the countryside and reduce the costs of providing services in every village. In the countryside around cities where the pressures for development are very strong, the policy seems to be quite effective in managing change, although there are circumstances where it is inappropriate, for example where there is an excess of top-tier growth centres, rather than a uniform spacing of larger and smaller villages, as seen in Fig. 4.23.

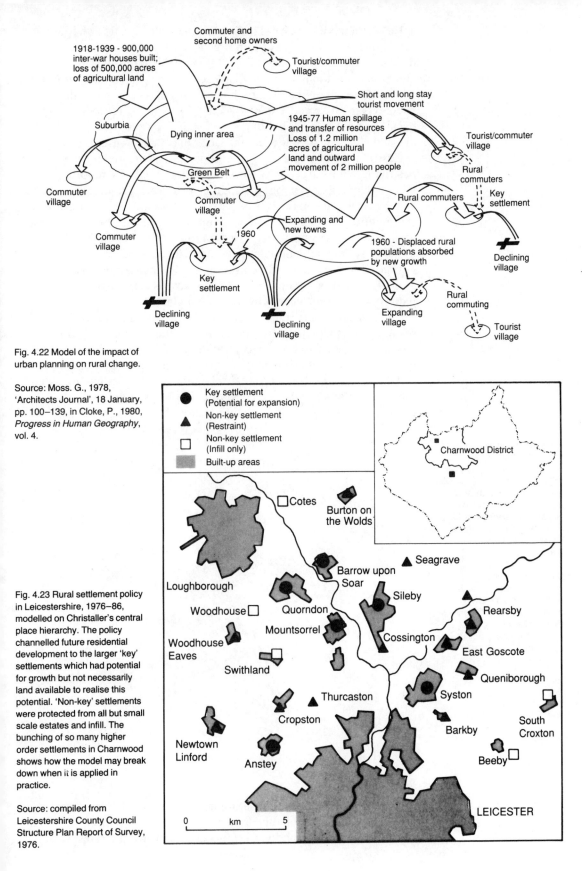

Fig. 4.22 Model of the impact of urban planning on rural change.

Source: Moss. G., 1978, 'Architects Journal', 18 January, pp. 100–139, in Cloke, P., 1980, *Progress in Human Geography*, vol. 4.

Fig. 4.23 Rural settlement policy in Leicestershire, 1976–86, modelled on Christaller's central place hierarchy. The policy channelled future residential development to the larger 'key' settlements which had potential for growth but not necessarily land available to realise this potential. 'Non-key' settlements were protected from all but small scale estates and infill. The bunching of so many higher order settlements in Charnwood shows how the model may break down when it is applied in practice.

Source: compiled from Leicestershire County Council Structure Plan Report of Survey, 1976.

85

Key settlement policy has influenced the scale, location and rate of rural housebuilding and has reinforced patterns of population distribution and migration (Fig. 4.24). Variable patterns of land release and estate development have influenced house prices and in turn the pattern of social segregation both between and within commuter villages (Fig. 4.25 and Tables 4.7 and 4.8). Housing for local people becomes more difficult to obtain as planning restrictions reduce land available for new building and the stock of council houses is sold.

Restrictive village planning of this kind is also blamed for the destruction of rural services. Several factors have been important: firstly, planning carried out by health and education authorities has had a dramatic impact on the spatial pattern of hospitals and schools (Humphries, 1977); secondly, economies of scale have been used as an argument for concentrating services in towns; thirdly, the greater mobility of the population has possibly reduced the demand, although not the need, for rural service provision. Rationalisation of services into a small number of larger centres has not always coincided with the pattern of change expected by settlement planners.

The concept of key settlement provides a starting point for analysing the impact of planning on the rural areas in the outer city regions. Essentially it is a form of 'concentration' model of how planners think urban change should be managed. Critics argue that key settlements are restrictive and inflexible. Strategic planning is out of fashion today and settlement planning will need new thinking if it is to deal with the pressures on the outer city – a point returned to in Chapter 5.

Fig. 4.24 Household mobility between and within 'key' settlements. The expansion of housing in selected 'key' centres may trigger off considerable population movement between and within settlements as this example from Leicestershire shows. But who moves where? And why?

Source: Herington, J., 1981, *Settlement policy and housing mobility*, Working Paper 6 for Economic and Social Research Council, Department of Geography, Loughborough University.

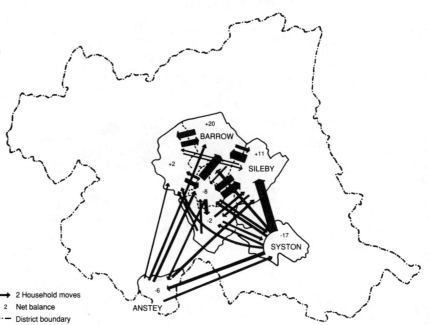

→ 2 Household moves
2 Net balance
—·— District boundary

Summary

Even well planned decentralisation was unlikely to please everyone. Middle-class interests in the Home Counties around London opposed some of the earliest London County Council overspill estates. Rural

Fig. 4.25 Privately built commuter housing in a Leicestershire 'key' village. The developer's advertisement board appeals to an idyllic image of village life and may attract those who can choose to live in the countryside.

Table 4.7 Socio-economic classification of occupations in commuter villages. The results of household surveys carried out in different regions at different times reveal a clear social stratification.

| Class | Description of occupations | Merseyside villages 1964[1] | | | Stratfield Mortimer 1962[2] | Bow Street 1964 | Milton Campsie 1977[3] |
		Greasby	Irby	Willaston			
I	Professional	13	8	22	3.6	9	17.3
II	Intermediate	37	37	11	19.4	25	31.8
III	Skilled	49	50	32	51.8	41	42.7
IV	Partly skilled	4	2	32	15.1	14	4.6
V	Unskilled	3	2	3	4.3	11	3.6
VI	Unclassified	—	1	—	5.8	—	—

Sources: 1 F. I. Masser and D.C. Stroud, 1965, 'The Metropolitan Village', *Town Planning Review*, no. 36, pp.111–124
2 R. Crichton, 1964, *Commuters' Village*, David and Charles, and Macdonald, p.26
3 M. Pacione, 1980, 'Quality of life in a metropolitan village, *Transactions Institute of British Geographers*, no. 50

Table 4.8 Social class of migrants to new dwellings in controlled commuter settlements, Leicestershire, 1977–80.

| Social class | Expanded villages | | Restrained villages | | Infill only villages | |
	% New	% All dwellings	% New	% All dwellings	% New	% All dwellings
I	11.6	6.5	22.2	15.2	16.7	11.4
II	27.4	24.6	51.9	36.1	50.0	59.1
III	56.8	60.0	25.9	42.8	33.3	27.3
IV	3.2	6.9	—	5.9	—	—
V	1.0	1.9	—	0.1	—	2.2
Total sample	(95)	(993)	(27)	(429)	(6)	(44)

Source: Herington, J. and Evans, D.M., 1980, '*The social characteristics of household movements in key and non-key settlements*', ESRC Research Project, Paper no.4, Dept. of Geography, Loughborough University.

'anti-growth' pressure groups found support from an alliance of countryside landowners, farmers and rural Counties, at a time when the protection of the agricultural industry was a primary government objective – very different from the agricultural surpluses of today. Containment was a compromise policy which sought to mediate between on the one hand the cities, hungry for land to meet their housing needs and increase rate intake and the countryside, anxious to safeguard farmland and amenity.

Containment has not been altogether successful. It was never possible to achieve a complete veto on all kinds of physical development in the outer city; for instance, major infrastructure projects, both motorways and airports, were sanctioned by central government and took extensive areas of open land and activated dispersal. The Green Belts, 'the jewel in the crown of the planning system', have held the floodgates back, but the Green Belt concept has begun to appear somewhat anachronistic in the 1980s as the circumstances which led to their creation have changed, that is, urban growth has gone beyond them. There have also been unintended social consequences to containment: Green Belts have proved socially regressive and the NTs and ETs have been unable to achieve the level of positive social discrimination their advocates hoped for. The poor have remained in the inner urban areas.

The very success of planned decentralisation has created unforeseen problems of urban management in the outer city regions. Urban expansion has often taken place beyond the size limits sought by central and local government. Boundary extensions have been common. Additional growth of jobs and housing has taken place in neighbouring settlements threatening containment objectives. The somewhat neglected problem of land availability has become more pressing as outer city regions attract major new infrastructure, for example the M42, M40, the fourth (and fifth?) terminal at Heathrow. Parts of the outer city suffer 'overheating' from too rapid urban growth. Swindon and Crawley are examples of planned towns bursting at the seams (Fig. 4.26).

C Regional economic development

Economic planning decisions have had an important effect upon regional development patterns. Government regional policy has been a significant driving force but it is important not to forget government investment in infrastructure, some of which is directly related to the attraction of industry, such as trading estates, but much of which has gone into motorway building, housing, derelict land clearance and commercial redevelopment. Although much infrastructure spending has been spatially directed toward improving the image of the Assisted Areas, a considerable amount has not been and indeed seems to have worked against regional policy aims, by enhancing the locational advantages of the already prosperous regions. The main elements of government planning are discussed below:

Regional policy

One of the key issues underpinning regional development policy has been the identification of realistic policy areas (Hunt Committee, 1967).

Fig. 4.26 The impact of planned dispersal on urban growth. Swindon was once an important railway centre. Since becoming an Expanded Town under the 1952 Town Development Act, the economic base and urban morphology of the town have changed dramatically. The photograph shows the new Central Business District and the rapid spread of new townships on greenfield sites well beyond the old limits of the town. *Source*: Aerofilms.

In the 1960s a variety of economic and social indicators could be used to show that Britain was a country divided into two nations roughly separated by the River Trent. The 'less prosperous regions', the North, Wales and Scotland, had higher than national rates of unemployment and low activity rates and out-migration of population. The 'more prosperous regions', covering the Midlands, South East and South West, all appeared to enjoy relative affluence. In the 1980s geographers are drawing attention to a continued social disparity in economic and social prosperity between North and South and between inner cities and prosperous rural areas (Fig. 4.27).

The primary tools of regional policy were the spatial and financial control of new manufacturing building in the prosperous regions. Firms wishing to expand beyond a certain specified floorspace limit needed to obtain an Industrial Development Certificate (IDC) as well as planning permission; these controls were coupled with labour subsidies and investment incentives for firms to relocate in less prosperous regions (a 'carrot and stick' approach). Office Development Permits (ODPs) were introduced in 1965 but their affect on long distance decentralisation of offices was limited. IDC controls were progressively tightened from about 1958 until the late 1970s and not until 1982, after a period of relaxation, were they eventually suspended. The amount of financial incentive ('carrots') available has varied over time and depended on which spatial classification of problem region the firm was moving to. The classifications have been changed with bewildering frequency over the years, as Hoare (1983) demonstrates (see Fig. 4.28).

The effects of controls over factory building have been both economic and physical and industrial location policies have had a significant influence on the inter-regional geography of economic activity in Britain. Keeble (1976) has argued that government policies 'must be accepted as the dominant reason for the recent shift in the balance of manufacturing locational advantage in favour of the periphery'.

Fig. 4.27 Changes in the unit price of housing (per sq.m of floorspace) 1982–86, shows a striking North–South divide. The data is collected for Local Labour Market Areas (LLMAs) which are defined as employment centres plus contiguous commuter hinterlands. There appears to be a 'ripple' effect as South East prices move northwards into the East Midlands. Substantial rises have also occured in smaller towns in parts of the North, whereas house price inflation has been lower in the West Midlands, west and north Wales and much of Scotland. The average price in 1986 exceeded £70 000 in the High Wycombe and Guildford areas.

Source: Champion, T. and Green, A., 1988, *Local Prosperity and the North–South Divide: Winners and Losers in 1980s Britain*, Coventry, Institute of Employment, Research, University of Warwick, and Nationwide Anglia Building Society.

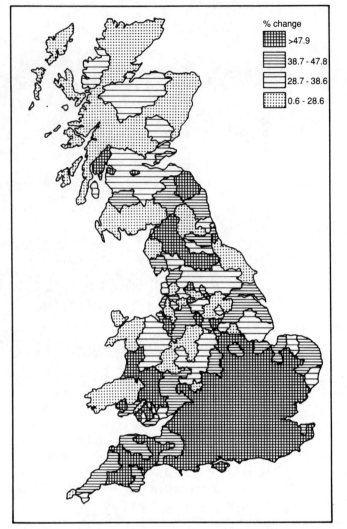

% change
▦ >47.9
▤ 38.7 - 47.8
▢ 28.7 - 38.6
▦ 0.6 - 28.6

Certainly, without government financial incentives and Industrial Development controls the level of manufacturing employment in the Assisted Areas would be considerably lower today. Fothergill and Gudgin (1982) estimate that between 1960 and 1979 manufacturing employment in the development regions rose by 184 000 or 10.8%, as a consequence of regional policy. The impact has been uneven. Scotland saw the largest total addition of manufacturing jobs, 57 000, but the smallest percentage change since 1960. On the other hand 53 000 manufacturing jobs were created in Wales, a 17.8% increase over the 1960 figure.

The spatial impacts of regional policy are evident in most of the assisted regions in the building of new factories and trading estates, often on the edge of towns and cities. In Wales the legacy of regional policy has made itself felt throughout the country. The Welsh Development Agency has constructed over 1000 factories since its formation in the mid-1970s and has begun new estates in districts affected by steel closures and the reclamation of derelict land. Electronic, audio and video equipment firms have expanded rapidly in the 1980s. Swansea has become one of Europe's largest video cassette centres. The WDA is now hoping to attract more high technology sectors of industry and is encouraging not just the provision of land, but

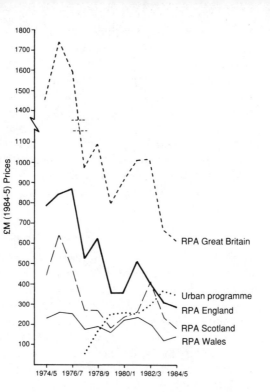

Fig. 4.28 Measuring the changing effect of government regional policy. Annual expenditure on Regional Preferential Assistance (RPA). The largest falls have been in English Assisted Areas whereas Scotland saw increased aid in the early 1980s targetted to oil-related companies. By 1984/5 spending on the cities was becoming more important than spending on the regions.

Source: Damesick, P. and Wood, P., 1987, *Regional Problems, Problem Regions and Public Policy in the UK*, Oxford, Oxford University Press, p.54.

improvements in the physical environment and development of technical skills among the local labour force. A further interesting point is that some very large plants, such as the Ford engine factory in South Wales, might not have come to Britain at all without regional aid.

Growth points

Another tool of regional development policy has been growth point planning. Growth points are settlements chosen by government for future public and private investment. When growth points were first used in Britain in the early 1960s it was argued that industries could not simply be expected to come to problem regions of their own accord – after all they were called problem regions because they lacked the economic advantages enjoyed by other areas. Nor were these advantages strictly economic in character. They covered the whole range of physical, social and environmental factors which influence industrial location: the provision of transport and communications networks, availability of industrial land and trading estates, housing for key workers and the workforce, the provision of social and recreational facilities, as well as an improved visual environment. In short, it was sensible to carry out comprehensive physical planning of locations if the economic planning for industrial location was to succeed. By channelling new investment on all these factors into just one or two growth locations, rather than spreading it thinly across the region, considerable savings in public expenditure might be achieved and selected centres were most likely to help revive peripheral economies.

Growth point planning has had important spatial and economic impacts. The concept has been applied extensively at all levels of planning decision-making in assisted and non-assisted regions (Fig. 4.29). Growth points have been used to help revive the sluggish

91

economies of problem regions, for example, Ireland, mid-Wales, the Highlands and Islands of Scotland and parts of Norfolk. In the early 1960s Central Scotland and north-east England were the first regions to see the official use of the growth point concept by central government. In many cases the selection of growth points has reflected the nodality of existing settlements, the availability of a large labour force and the perceived opportunities for industrial expansion. Although NTS were primarily intended for the relief of population pressures in the major cities, they have sometimes been defined with the purpose of promoting regional development for example. Central Lancashire NT in north west England and Newtown in mid-Wales.

Assisted areas and growth points in the 1980s

Although government expenditure on regional preferential assistance has fallen in real terms by 40% from the level of the mid-1970s, some regions continue to attract new industrial investment. The inter-relationship between regional policy and growth points is well illustrated among the large international organisations from Japan and America, whose decision to expand in Development Areas has depended largely on the level of government grants available and the infrastructure found in growth points. The so-called 'Silicon Glen' in Scotland (Table 4.9) has attracted a cluster of high-technology electronics industries which employ over 40 000 people. In 1983 a £40m

Table 4.9 Silicon Glen jobs and investment 1980–84. The New Towns attracted a substantial share of new high technology investment in Central Scotland.

New Towns in Central Scotland	% Jobs in electronics	% Investment in electronics
Livingston	19.3	18.4
Glenrothes	14.8	6.8
East Kilbride	8.1	17.6
Irvine	5.2	1.1
	47.4	43.9
Other locations:		
Greenock	25.9	40.4
Edinburgh	11.9	3.0
Stirling	6.9	8.1
Airdrie/Newhouse	4.5	1.5
Glasgow	3.3	3.0
	52.5	56.0

Source: adapted from *Sunday Times*, 11 November 1984

Nippon Electric microchip assembly plant was opened at Livingston NT. The decision by Nissan, the Japanese car manufacturer, to build its British plant at the former Sunderland airport site at Washington NT, reflects both the continued political importance of government regional policy and the promotional activities of the NT Corporation in seeking new jobs. Nissan will initially employ between 400 and 500 people in assembling cars from kits sent from Japan and ultimately employment may increase to 2000.

Fig. 4.29 Impact of a growth point on industrial activity. Ironically many of these firms have been attracted to Peterborough without the benefit of regional grant aid. More important factors have been the availability of labour, land and buildings with modern infrastructure, as well as the locational advantages of Peterborough close to London.

Source: Peterborough Development Corporation

THE COMPANIES WHO'VE MOVED THEIR BUSINESSES TO PETERBOROUGH ARE LEGION.

THERM-A-STOR

CROSFIELD ELECTRONICS

THOMAS COOK

VNITED TECHNOLOGIES

MARKS & SPENCER

ROYAL LIFE

BRITISH SVGAR

HOTPOINT

PEARL ASSVRANCE

TSB

Since 1970, over 500 companies have moved to Peterborough including Acco, United Technologies, Precision Valve and Dyna Five from the US.

Peterborough today is a unique blend of the traditional and the most modern, the ideal choice for companies seeking a new location.

Premises and sites are ready now, at very competitive costs.

There's an outstanding choice of housing. Schools are first class andpeople here enjoy unrivalled sporting and recreational opportunities.

Peterborough is just 50 minutes by high speed 125 train (and 78 miles up the A1) from London. It has excellent connections with the North, the Midlands, and the expanding East Coast ports.

If you'd like to join the legions, make sure of your free complete guide to relocation. Fill in and return the coupon, or call John Bouldin on Peterborough (0733) 68931.

To:
John Bouldin, Peterborough Development Corporation, Stuart House, City Road, Peterborough PE1 1UJ. Please send me your free complete guide to relocation.

Name

Position

Company

Address

Tel

THE PETERBOROVGH EFFECT

IT'S BEEN WORKING FOR CENTVRIES.

93

Changing tactics   Regional policy has been modified over time to suit changing economic conditions and perceived political priorities. During the 1970s, due to widespread economic recession and increased unemployment in all regions, the government decided to be much more selective in its approach (Townsend, 1980). In 1983 they eliminated Special Development Areas and cut back the extent of Development Areas in Scotland, Wales and northern England.

One very significant change was made: a traditionally prosperous urban region, the West Midlands, acquired problem status for the first time (see Fig. 4.30).

Regional policies in the post-war decades were formulated against a distinctive geography of unemployment. The aim was to help areas of high unemployment by encouraging industry to move away from regions like the West Midlands and the South East, which were then enjoying continued economic expansion. By the mid-1970s there had been a significant shift in the spatial incidence of high unemployment. Some inner cores of previously prosperous regions began to feel the effects of decline in their manufacturing base. The West Midlands was a case in point. Between 1974 and 1982 the region lost 33% of its manufacturing jobs, a rate of decline exceeded only by Wales (-34%). Unemployment increased very rapidly after 1979 and reached 17% by September 1982. The new distribution of unemployment revealed a further dimension: the inner areas of London and Birmingham, previously regarded as the prosperous regions, were hit as hard by high unemployment as the northern conurbations. Indeed, absolute levels of those out of work in London were found to be equivalent to those in the whole of Scotland. Clearly high unemployment was as much 'urban' as 'regional' in character. The government responded by shifting the focus of spatial policy towards the inner cities.

Assisting the urban economy

Specific measures were suggested in the White Paper on Policy for the Inner Cities and introduced in the Inner Urban Areas Act, 1978. They included the setting up of Partnership Areas in Lambeth, Islington–Hackney and Docklands in London, Newcastle–Gateshead, Manchester–Salford, Liverpool and Birmingham. Their purpose was to combine central and local government action for economic regeneration. Various 'designated districts', equivalent in status to Assisted Areas, were able to receive financial incentives. The Partnership Areas were given second priority to the Assisted Areas in the granting of IDCs and before the NTs and non-Assisted Areas. The policy of the London Office Bureau (LOB) was completely turned around, from encouragement to discouragement of office decentralisation.

The Enterprise Zone (EZ) concept was introduced to help provide employment in some of the worst problem areas. EZs are small areas (less than 250 hectares) offering certain freedoms (similar to those available under regional policy) to industrialists as a 'carrot' to locate: for example, exemptions from taxes and rates on property, no requirements to obtain planning permission. The EZs were treated by the government as an experiment in deregulation, on the assumption that too much control was the reason why industry was not seeking to locate in the older industrial areas. Ironically many of the defined sites

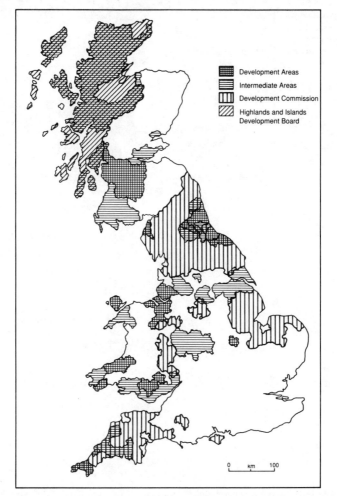

Fig. 4.30 Regional Assisted
Areas and Rural Development
Agencies, 1988. The areas
covered by the development
agencies are greater than the
presently assisted areas.

Sources: Department of Trade
and Industry Current Planning
Issues

Development Areas
Intermediate Areas
Development Commission
Highlands and Islands
Development Board

0   km   100

have been located outside the major conurbations, for instance at
Invergordan, Telford and Corby (see Fig. 4.31) emphasising the nature
of EZs as a response to particular local employment crises, rather than
any coherent strategy for dealing with the urban problem. One effect of
Enterprise Zones has been to attract developments which have
commonly experienced difficulty in obtaining planning approval, for
example, large scale retail enterprises (see Chapter 3).

The intention behind the 1978 Inner Areas Act was that the main
components of national planning policy, land-use control, housing and
industrial location policy, should be directed toward the inner urban
areas, while dispersal was to be given lower priority. The Thatcher
government announced new measures for co-ordinating inner city
policy in 1988, with the intention of attracting private sector funding for
economic regeneration. However this package seems to rule out any
radically different national urban policy.

Non-spatial planning policies

While regional development patterns are most obviously influenced by
government policy for industrial location and growth points, there are
many other national government planning actions which have important
spatial impacts. These are of two kinds: firstly, the direct and obvious
spatial consequences resulting from government ownership or control

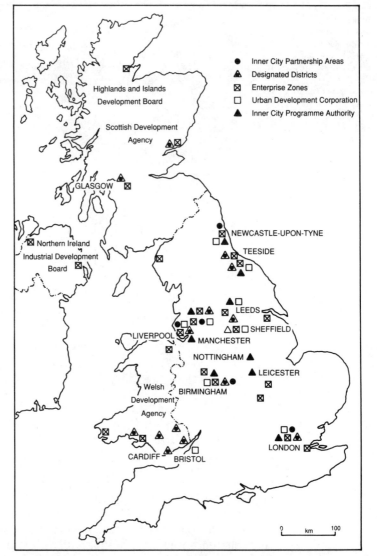

Fig. 4.31 Government sponsored urban economic initiatives. The localised and complex pattern cuts across the traditional pattern of aid to the regions, reflecting the various policies of the Department of the Environment and the Department of Enterprise.

Source: adapted from Damesick and Wood, p.52. (see Fig. 4.28.)

of industry, as in the case of British Leyland, British Shipbuilders or British Steel. Government is a major determinant of the location of investment and, increasingly, of disinvestment. The West Midlands, traditionally a non-assisted area, benefitted over many years from the large amounts of government aid given to British Leyland and therefore suffered when public funds were withdrawn. The impact of steel closures on the economic geography of problem regions has been dramatic: for instance, 20 000 jobs in steel were lost in South Wales between 1976 and 1980.

Secondly, the spending and investment decisions of central government departments, whilst not guided by any particular spatial planning policy, have very important implications for regional development, which may run against regional policy aims. The role of government in channelling aid to 'high-technology' sectors of the defence and aerospace industries is a good illustration of this. The industries that are vital for defence (communications, electronics, aerospace) were originally concentrated in the south. The government decided to site many defence research establishments to the west of London and in the corridor between Bristol and London. When analysed on a regional basis, Table 4.10 indicates that government defence spending is most important to the economy of the South East and to a lesser extent the South West. Interestingly, the size of defence procurement grants greatly exceeds that of regional aid grants. Furthermore, the regions which gain most from defence expenditure are precisely those regions where the economies are already booming.

Table 4.10 Defence procurement and regional aid grants by region, 1977–8, (£ million).

	Defence procurement contracts	Regional Aid Grants
	£m	£m
North	174.2	142.3
Yorkshire/Humberside	61.9	26.7
East Midlands	213.2	1.4
East Anglia	111.7	—
South East	1175.6	—
South West	410.2	7.8
West Midlands	189.2	—
North West	242.8	57.6
Wales	25.6	74.4
Scotland	195.0	113.1
Northern Ireland	27.9	50.1

Notes

(i) Defence procurement contracts include: the purchase of defence hardware for air, land and sea systems; clothing and textiles; liquids, fuels, lubricants etc.; research; contract repair of ships and vessels.

(ii) Regional Aid Grants include Regional Development Grants (paid under the Industry Act, 1972) and selective assistance grants. Note that the East and West Midlands together received £0.5m in selective assistance grants which are not included in the table. For Northern Ireland the grant figures are for Investment and capital grants and Industrial Development Grants.

Source: Short, 1981a, 1981b, Regional Statistics 1978, 1979

Transport infrastructure

Central government has also played a crucial role in transport planning (see Chapter 3). The improvement in accessibility which follows the construction of new motorways has activated institutional investment in regional development. Nowhere are these effects more evident that in the south east of England. The motorways radiating from London have now been intersected by the completion of the M25, a 194 kilometre motorway which encircles 8 million people. The building of the M25 has strengthened the South East's nodal position in the transport network of Britain and the European Economic Community and consequently the region's advantages for development. The comparative advantages to industry and commerce of locating near motorway junctions on the M25, or the settlements beyond, have increased. This is apparent from the desire of property investors to seek locations in the western crescent of the M25 ring, notably between the A3 and A1. In addition, the M11 is seen to have enhanced the attraction for property investment in the 1990s (Hall et al., 1986) although the M3 and M4 corridors seem likely to retain their importance to the investment market (Fig. 4.32).

Fig. 4.32 Motorway corridors:
potential rental growth in
property investment as
perceived by institutional
investors, 1987 (sample of 250).

Source: compiled from Derrick,
Wade and Waters, 1987,
*Property Investment Intentions:
A Financial Survey*, London,
Derrick, Wade and Waters,
29a Wimpole Street.

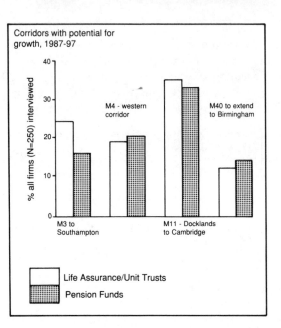

Case study: corridor developments in the South East

Economic activity is moving away from major urban areas out towards
suburban and rural areas. However the outer areas of greatest relative
advantage for industrial location have a distinct corridor bias. This is
because good accessibility is an important locating factor for modern
industry. Improved accessibility is the outcome of government
investment in road, rail and air transport links (see Fig. 4.33). What is
interesting about these corridor development patterns, is that they
demonstrate the combined effects of different scales of planning
decision-making and their interaction with traditional economic
location factors: national programmes for transport and defence
expenditure, regional growth points and local authority economic plans.

The M3 and M4 corridors and M27 were characterised by rapid
development of modern industries over the period 1976–86. These
include some of those mentioned above in the context of government
defence expenditure and, in addition, pharmaceutical chemicals,
electronic computers, telephone equipment, radio and radar goods.
The spatial pattern of employment associated with this trend in the so-
called Western Corridor between London and Bristol is far from
uniform. The core of high-technology activity, particularly electronics,
is at the London end of the M4 corridor, in Berkshire, Hampshire and
Hertfordshire. Areas further west, Wiltshire and Avon, have not joined
in the M4 phenomenon to the same extent, nor has South Wales. The
major settlements experiencing growth in employment up to 1981 were
Bracknell, Reading and Portsmouth. Swansea enjoyed a small but
significant gain in an area of general high-tech decline. Perhaps most
surprising has been the growth of the manufacturing sector in South
Hampshire, in marked contrast to many Development Areas and to
national trends. In the 10 years to 1981 the number of jobs in South
Hampshire grew by 6.6% while the total for Britain fell by 1.3%.

It would be misleading to attribute the regional development of this
part of the South East entirely to government planning. The main
factors of importance for firms locating in the eastern part of the M4

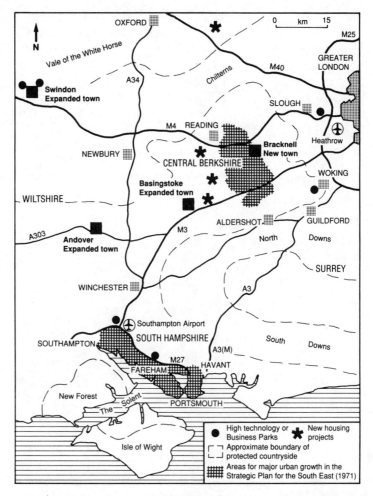

Fig. 4.33 Corridor development in south east England. State investment in motorways, the expansion of Heathrow Airport and the building of New and Expanded Towns, as well as the planned protection of the countryside, have all helped to attract employment and population dispersal along these corridors.

corridor or the Thames Valley have been found to be skilled labour, a pleasant environment and good communications, particularly links with local customers and suitable premises. The attraction of the M3 and M27 corridors can be attributed to similar perceived advantages, especially cheaper sites for expansion (when compared to London locations) and the opportunity for firms to locate near attractive environments like the New Forest or the Solent, with their obvious recreational advantages, together with the favourable climate compared to some other parts of the UK. However, underpinning many of these apparently 'natural' economic endowments lie the all pervasive influences of direct and indirect government planning, namely:

(a) *national regional policy*   Location of industry policy has had a considerable impact on the expanding electrical engineering and electronics industries. It appears that possibly because of their importance for defence, electronic factories found it easy to obtain IDCs in the prosperous South East and the overspill towns near London. Fig. 4.34 demonstrates the importance of the Solent's role in Britain's maritime defence, particularly in the Portsmouth area. Large defence related electronics firms are found located on or near the M27. The Ministry of Defence employs about 60 000 people in this area and is by far the largest employer. The LOB has played a role in corridor development by promoting cheaper and more suitable locations outside London, particularly in NTs and ETs, which have then become magnets for office and high technology expansion.

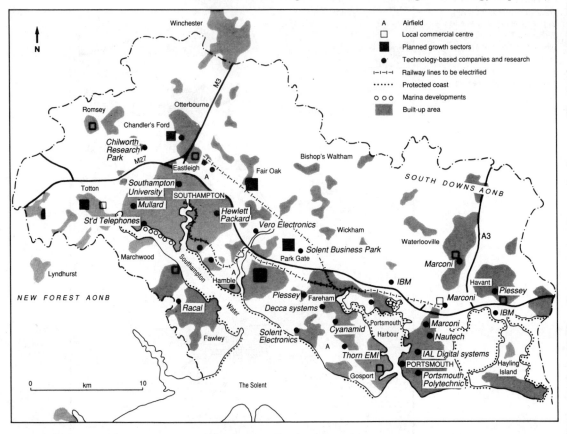

Fig. 4.34 British Silicon Valley along the M27. The relationship between State and capital investment is shown.

Source: constructed from *Sunday Times*

(b) growth points The growth points planned around London were aimed as much at the relief of population pressures on the capital as on job dispersal. But they have altered the spatial patterns of employment especially in the service (offices) sector and it is not surprising to find that the places now sought after for industrial development are those which have been subject to comprehensive planning over a long period. Bracknell, designated a NT in 1951, has seen major growth of office development diverted from central London. Basingstoke, a London overspill town of the 1960s, has experienced an office development boom, which is clearly visible to the traveller passing along the M3 in the form of high-rise blue-glass office buildings (Fig. 4.35). Furthermore, in the regional strategic planning proposals for south east England since 1964, South Hampshire, Central Berkshire and Swindon have been singled out as locations for major future urban expansion (see Fig. 4.33). The subsequent South Hampshire Plan and other local authority planning policies have guided the release of land for large scale housebuilding at places like Chandlers Ford and Totton, thus ensuring the rapid urbanisation of the M27 corridor. Similarly Swindon, designated an Expanded Town under the 1952 Town Development Act, was specifically earmarked for major expansion in the regional plans for the South East. It has subsequently seen an expansion of high technology and electronics firms attracted by urban and infrastructure development, despite the absence of regional aid (Fig. 4.26).

(c) transport planning Transport planning acts as a strong catalyst for modern industry. The effect of motorways on the corridor distribution of new industry is clearly noted where the local planning authorities have granted permission for 'science' or 'business parks'. The parks specialise in micro-electronics, robotics, computer and other forms of information technology and are characterised by low density layout of buildings and park-like settings. Despite the lack of regional aid, private and public developers, often in partnership, find it advantageous to locate near the motorways. The private developers of the Solent Business Park, off junction 9 of the M27 midway between Southampton and Portsmouth, expect to create 7000 jobs in science-based firms. Hampshire County Council has reserved sites for 'large space users'

Fig. 4.35 Basingstoke boom town: new business and office developments have grown rapidly on land between housing areas and the M3. *Source*: Basingstoke Gazette.

to the west of Southampton taking advantage of the M27. In addition, Hewlett Packard, Thamesdown Borough Council and Taylor Woodrow Property Company have been active building new factory floorspace on sites close to the M4 on the edge of Swindon.

Summary

One important effect of government investment in infrastructure in the South East is the stimulus it generates for further physical expansion and economic growth in the region. The M25 and Channel Tunnel project will reinforce the tendency for wealth concentration in the South. Would it be preferable to strengthen regional policy and try to reduce regional disparities, or to adopt a policy of allowing industry to maximise the growth potential offered by the new communications and airports in the South East? The costs of over-rapid economic development in the South East (e.g. excessive house prices and traffic congestion) may encourage firms to look elsewhere for expansion. If this happens we may see a renewed government interest in the planned development of other regions.

101

5 A changing role for planning

Political theory has changed radically since the inter-war years when planning was in its infancy. In those days people viewed the State more or less as a benevolent provider of goods and services. Today, the desirability of the State as provider of welfare and controller of the public interest is questioned. Powerful capitalist interests and popular opinion challenge the principle of State intervention in social affairs and in doing so reach the heart of spatial and economic planning. The very purposes of State planning are questioned. Is planning necessary any more? If so, what role should it play in society? This chapter looks at the changing role of planning in society. It extends the themes raised in earlier chapters, since we briefly examine why planning as a process of decision-making is changing, what new kinds of geographical conflict arise and what the geographical consequences may be. The planning of housing and residential development is used to illustrate these themes.

Why is planning under attack?

Some of the arguments in favour of planning were outlined briefly in Chapter 1. Almost every advanced capitalist economy has seen it necessary to have a planning system for regulating land development. Planning would appear to be here to stay and any attempt to seriously dismantle development planning and control would seem likely to arouse fierce political opposition. However, the function of planning in a modern society depends at any time on the powers given to it by Parliament and prevailing social attitudes toward public intervention in the private sector of the economy.

Changing political objectives – the State in retreat

In the book *Garden Cities of Tomorrow*, Ebenezer Howard argued that for planning to be effective the community should be given the power to make decisions about its future. For the community to obtain power, it would first have to own the land on which a city was to be built and then it would be entitled to the wealth created in the 'assets' (factories, houses, roads). In practical terms this meant that private ownership of land would be inconsistent with government of the community. This principle was enshrined in the New Town Act, 1946, in which the ownership of new towns was vested in state bodies known as Development Corporations and has not been forgotten in the recently founded Urban Development Corporations.

The founders of planning expected the State to play the key role in promoting the scale, location and kind of urban development. In practice, the private sector has increased its influence over the planning process during the period since World War II. In Britain, unlike

Sweden for example, most development land has remained in private hands and thus spatial planning has lacked the power to initiate urban development or directly provide for certain social groups. Much spatial planning control appears to respond to, rather than lead, events, although it is important not to forget that even reactive planning will limit the influence of developers. Planners still possess the power to identify land for development in plans and to control development change through use of planning legislation (i.e. 1947 Town and Country Planning Act). It is the exercise of these powers within the political system which has become more difficult as right-wing critics of planning have accused it of being a bureaucratic irrelevance to free enterprise.

Furthermore, in recent times the wealth of the assets created by the State in the form of factories and houses has been sold off to the private sector rather than being returned to the local community in the way Howard would have liked. For a long time it was accepted that the State should be entitled to a share of the personal increase in the value of land which may result from a particular piece of land being zoned in a development plan, or as a consequence of a planning permission. Taxation of the profits to be made from increased development value (betterment) has been central to Labour governments' approaches to planning, for example the Land Commission, 1967 the Community Land Act 1975 and Conservative administrations have also, at least until 1985, subscribed to the need for this form of taxation.

The emerging centre stage for decision-making

Recent Conservative governments in Britain have been anxious to reduce the role of the State in the management of the space economy, because of their belief that the State inhibits private enterprise. Planning powers have been decentralised from one level of local government (Counties) to another (Districts). One level of strategic planning decision-making, carried out by the Metropolitan Counties, was abolished in April 1986, primarily in the interests of fiscal efficiency (Department of the Environment, 1983). However, contrary to what might be expected from these examples, a greater degree of centralised decision-making has proved necessary in handling the relationships between national and local levels of planning (see the 'top-down' model in Chapter 2). For instance, Labour controlled councils in the inner cities have been blamed for excessive public spending and some Conservative councils admonished for dragging their heels in providing houses where people want to live. Spatial planning appears to have become less of a political priority than the housebuilding industry, because building houses is the route toward higher levels of owner-occupation and a 'property owning democracy'.

The increased power of corporate interests

One explanation for a more permissive national approach to urban development is the shared national political interest of the development industry and the present (1988) Conservative government. This relationship between two powerful groups of decision-makers tends to dominate government attitudes towards planning decision-making at all levels. In contrast the period before the 1970s was characterised by less dominant national power blocks and a strong alliance between farming and landowning interests with local government stronger in keeping out unwanted urban change.

Local planning organisations have to respond to the pressures of increasingly well-mobilised business and capital organisations. Multinational companies have proved a dominant force. Decision-making has become concentrated at higher levels of industry: the production strategies of the largest companies will be decided without much apparent reference to spatial consequences. Disinvestment may leave abandoned buildings and waste land and require remedial local economic and spatial planning, while investment may bring about the destruction of the countryside and the decay of the cities. Local planning has begun to seem a form of 'crisis management', forced to respond to these external events and decisions.

Professional planners have in turn begun to address their future role in society. Should they remain physical planners, essentially involved in the output of decisions which have been made by non-government agencies? Or should they become more directly involved in the economic decision-making process of these agencies? More are becoming advisors to the private sector, joining major housing, retailing and commercial companies and thus seeking to influence land development policy at an early stage in the decision process (Fig. 5.1).

Fig. 5.1 Sign of the times: an advertisement in a planning journal. The scope and size of planning consultancy has grown dramatically in recent years.

The agricultural land crisis

Government policy has long been committed to the principle of urban containment and the protection of agriculture. But planning policies for the countryside are in a state of flux because of the controversy about surplus agricultural land. A possible 1.2–1.6 million hectares of farmland could be released from farming, but what is the best alternative use of land? Some interests would wish to see a more dispersed pattern of urban activity, including housing and factories in smaller settlements, with the best quality farmland still protected.

Others prefer to see farmland protection maintained, if not to serve the agricultural industry, to conserve the countryside as an important national resource for nature conservation, recreation, leisure, tourism and amenity (Countryside Commission, 1987). The debate is raging in 1987 and the direction any new national land-use policy may take is uncertain. The geographical consequences of a rethink on land-use protection could be very dramatic even over a relatively short time-scale.

Planning goals today

A convenient though rather over-simplified distinction is sometimes made in the planning literature between the social, physical and economic goals of planning (see, for instance, Bruton, 1981). Put simply, the goal of spatial planning is the orderly arrangement of land and buildings to suit changing social, economic and technological demands. Social planning has sought to achieve a degree of 'social balance' in town development, that is, the integration of people from all socio-economic categories within a defined area. This element in spatial planning is becoming less fashionable although changing life styles are placing a new emphasis on the quality and design of new housing environments for those able to move. The desire of local communities to see their environment protected has also become an important social and political concern. Economic goals are widening the opportunities for free enterprise, often through the provision of communications and industrial land and buildings, as for instance in the frenetic activities of many local authorities to attract new industry to their area (Fig. 5.2).

(a) Social and environmental goals

Few planners would claim that they could change society, although many would accept their capacity to influence social change. Spatial planning seems a rather blunt instrument for achieving an improved distribution of wealth in society, since this will depend on factors beyond the control of planners, for instance, the general level of economic welfare and government social support to groups in general or particular. For spatial planners to provide for the needs of the poor would require much greater control over the production process and the provision of social investment in different areas. Nonetheless, many politicians and members of the public agree that the provision of employment and decent housing are fundamental social priorities and that the physical planner should, insofar as is possible, take such factors into account in formulating urban plans.

The phasing, design and layout of New Towns has been controlled by State owned development corporations. Weight has been given to social goals, with the physical arrangement of land-use, aesthetics and better living environments being seen as a means for achieving social aims. The relationship between social and spatial planning goals is well illustrated in the planning of New Towns. But some social goals may seem too ambitious today. The rather crude assumption that physical form will determine social behaviour is questioned. Which comes first? Do people change their surroundings or do surroundings change people?

Fig. 5.2 Motorway junctions are especially attractive for certain kinds of industry, if planning policies permit – Meridian Business Park, Leicester.

'A simple causal relationship between environment and social behaviour does not exist. The neighbourhood unit was found to be larger than the neighbourhood community. Social integration tended to foster rather than reduce social segregation. Once the irreconcilability of certain social and physical planning goals was recognised a reaction against neighbourhood planning set in. This reaction has now been succeeded by a more cautious approach characterized by an awareness of social process that may or may not be related to the physical environment'
(Blowers, 1981).

Social goals underpin all land-use management. The general public interest, insofar as this can be defined, would seem to benefit enormously from attractive living and working environments. In a sense, all of us gain from a protected countryside. Nonetheless, while the environmental gains from having planning should never be underestimated, these general advantages have been achieved at the expense of the less well-off (Hall, 1973; Reade, 1987). This raises interesting points for debate: whose interest should planning serve? How important is a carefully planned physical environment to those without a job? Private landowners and business interests will make considerable financial gain from the increase in development value following planning permission. But those households on low incomes find house prices high in Green Belts. Small businesses may gain over large national companies in a situation where the supply of development sites is limited and so on. All this confirms that planning has socially redistributive effects, although these are not always in the direction intended by planners. One critical view of the social effects of planning is given by the geographer Peter Ambrose (1986):

'Planning, and the present piecemeal removal of it in the interests of powerful minority groups, is a wealth-redistributive mechanism. Structure Plans and Local Plans create new maps of land value, producing vast extra wealth for some landowners and none for others'
(Ambrose, p. 276).

(b) Wealth-creation goals

Unguided market forces radically changed the faces of cities and regions in the first third of the twentieth century. From these trends grew a consensus of political opinion in favour of planning as a radical alternative economic strategy for managing land, labour and capital. In 1988, market forces are to be encouraged rather than restrained and the time for a restrictive, negative style of physical planning appears to have come to an end. Wealth creation is a political priority and the purposes of spatial planning have been redefined to enable free enterprise to build where it chooses.

The 1980s have witnessed a major overhaul of the development plan and the control system. Many County Structure Plans have been regarded as too restrictive to free enterprise, with the result that their population and housing targets have been increased by the Secretary of State for the Environment. National policy guidance to local planning authorities has also been changed, sometimes in rather subtle ways, to facilitate private production (see Circular 22/80). Local government planners have been told by central government to provide houses where people want to live. This is easier said than done. Some Counties have restrictive policies while others are much more permissive; many District planning committees do not want to be swamped by new housing development. Moreover, there are well established national policies, like the Green Belt, which would be directly challenged if builders were allowed to meet demand in the most profitable locations.

What will be the result of these wealth creating goals for the geography of the 1990s? The most dynamic areas for industrial and commercial development seem likely to remain the outer parts of the regional city. Changing life-styles, new uses for farmland and buildings, committed government investment in transport infrastructure, the further relaxation of physical planning and many other factors suggest the 'spread city' shown in Fig. 5.3 must be one possible scenario for the future.

The problem with this model is that it assumes a political consensus in favour of dispersal. Although 1980s government policy is geared toward economic development, it also attempts to constrain development on environmental grounds. The occasion for conflict over the scale and location of future housing increases as government wealth-creating priorities clash head on with the priorities of local government and the environmentalists, who still adhere to the tenets of urban containment. Large and even small releases of greenfield land for housebuilding, even in non-Green Belt locations, may prove politically contentious, even under a non-interventionist government and despite the more ready availability of farmland. New forms of high-technology industry, science and business parks or leisure centres which are employment-generating, may prove more acceptable.

Achieving wealth-creating goals is more difficult in the inner cities. These areas will not attract private industry without the necessary infrastructure in communications and public utilities (water supply, sewerage) and the State must play a part in subsidising these facilities if it wishes to make the inner cities more attractive for private industry. The Enterprise Zones and Urban Development Corporations announced in the Local Government, Planning and Land Act, 1980, may succeed in attracting private capital but given the absence of any

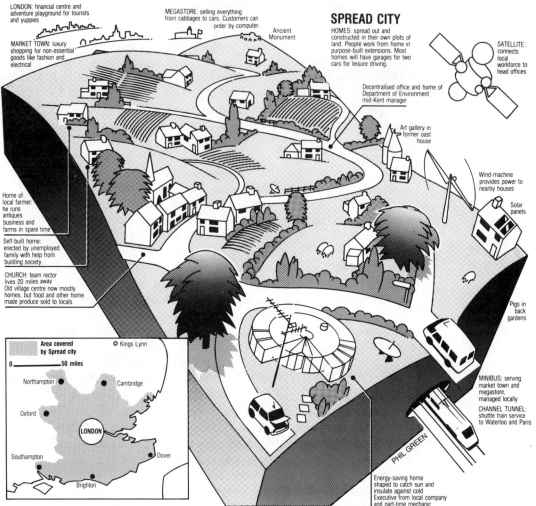

SPREAD CITY

LONDON: financial centre and adventure playground for tourists and yuppies

MARKET TOWN: luxury shopping for non-essential goods like fashion and electrical

MEGASTORE: selling everything from cabbages to cars. Customers can order by computer.

Ancient Monument

HOMES: spread out and constructed in their own plots of land. People work from home in purpose-built extensions. Most homes will have garages for two cars for leisure driving.

SATELLITE: connects local workforce to head offices

Decentralised office and home of Department of Environment mid-Kent manager

Art gallery in former oast house

Wind-machine provides power to nearby houses

Solar panels

Home of local farmer: he runs antiques business and farms in spare time

Self-built home: erected by unemployed family with help from building society

CHURCH: team rector lives 20 miles away Old village centre now mostly homes, but food and other home made produce sold to locals

Pigs in back gardens

Area covered by Spread city

○ Kings Lynn

0 ———— 50 miles

Northampton

Cambridge

Oxford

LONDON

Southampton

Dover

Brighton

MINIBUS: serving market town and megastore, managed locally

CHANNEL TUNNEL: shuttle train service to Waterloo and Paris

PHIL GREEN

Energy-saving home shaped to catch sun and insulate against cold Executive from local company and part-time mechanic

Fig. 5.3 Spread City. In this vision of the future there will be less land devoted to agriculture, new uses for farmland and buildings, small scale enterprises, conservation of the landscape and new forms of dispersed urban settlement.

Source: *Sunday Times*

Fig. 5.4 Private enterprise in the inner city: the Docklands Light Railway, opened in 1987, has been financed by Olympia and York, the company developing Canary Wharf with the LDDC and London Regional Transport. *Source*: London Docklands Development Corporation.

effective regional policy, their successes are likely to be greater in those inner areas which have the greatest locational advantages, for example London compared to Liverpool (Figs. 5.4 and 5.5).

The relationship between inner city and regional policy seems likely to remain ambivalent. Neither set of government initiatives can be justified solely as 'wealth creation'. Both aim to restructure the economic base by attracting new kinds of high-technology or diversified industry. The regional policy pronouncements of 1984 refer to the relief

Fig. 5.5 New uses for Royal Docks: the newly completed City Airport for Short Take Off and Landing (STOL) with the skyline of the City of London in the background. *Source*: Rex Features Ltd.

of unemployment as a social necessity rather than economic imperative. Putting new industries into poorer regions may effect a better distribution of employment opportunity between regions and this could be interpreted as a desirable social, rather than strictly economic, gain. In addition, the 1987 General Election results produced a new spatial map of voting patterns. The inner cities, the north of England and Scotland, in particular, did not support the policies of Thatcher's government. In my opinion, recent planning approaches must also be seen as an attempt to secure a foothold for Conservatism in traditional Labour strongholds.

Summary

National economic performance and industrial efficiency were not the aims which motivated the founders of planning, people like Ebenezer Howard and Patrick Geddes. Their concern was much more with the social and physical form of the build environment and the inequalities in prosperity between people living in different places. In the 1980s, spatial planning is being turned toward these new economic imperatives, while some of the social concerns are neglected.

The new style of planning sits uneasily within the radical and idealistic philosophy of the past. A few planners still argue that the roots of their profession go back to the social crusading of the early visionaries like Howard. They find it difficult to justify their role in terms of helping free enterprise to flourish. But contemporary spatial planning policies are geared closely to the needs of the economy and the generation of employment. Some question whether this is really 'planning' in the old sense, but rather a form of economic management involving a mixture of complementary, though different, planning roles.

Conflicting goals – a case study

In Chapter 3 reference was made to the problems of conflict arising from the interplay of divergent interests in the planning process. How are the changing planning goals discussed above interpreted today? Is the balance of power moving away from the planner to the developer? Answers to these questions will depend on which examples are used. The following case is interesting because it is the first of its kind in recent years, where a major housebuilding project has directly challenged Green Belt policy.

A rather complex set of circumstances has encouraged the private sector to build completely new settlements in the open countryside. Some of these have already been sanctioned by local planning authorities. The South East has witnessed most of this activity, but other regions have seen new private town developments (Fig. 5.6). In 1985, seven of Britain's biggest housebuilders, Tarmac, Barratt, Wimpey, Ideal Homes, Beazer, Bovis and Wilcon, proposed building a new 'country town' for 15 000 people in the London Green Belt at

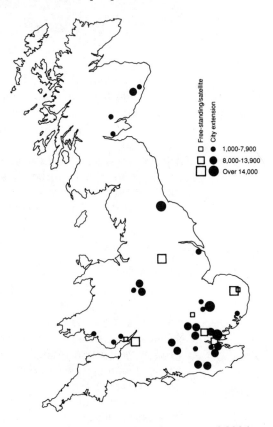

Fig. 5.6 Private sector new settlements in the countryside. The South East accounts for the majority of schemes, a reflection of intense housing demands and limited housing land.

Source: constructed from data contained in *Town and Country Planning*, November 1986.

Tillingham Hall, near Grays, Essex. The site covered 300 hectares of flat and rather uninspiring farmland landscape located in the middle of an eight kilometre stretch of country that provided a gap between otherwise nearly continuous building from London to Southend (Fig. 5.7).

All the key interests were represented in the ensuing conflict. Firstly, Essex County Council and the then Greater London Council challenged the housebuilders' assumptions on housing need; secondly, national and local environmental interests were fiercely hostile to building in the Green Belt (Fig. 5.8). Central government was called in to mediate between the conflicts of interest.

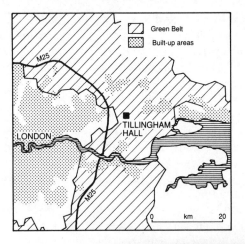

Fig. 5.7 Tillingham Hall site.

Green Belt

Built-up areas

Fig. 5.8 Tillingham Hall: the environmental protest group toast a successful campaign. Source: Echo Newspapers.

Four key issues were disputed at the public inquiry:

1 **Housing demand**. The builders claimed a need for 880 000 dwellings in south east England by 1991 whereas the Department of the Environment and SERPLAN, a consultative regional grouping of Shire counties, the GLC and the London Boroughs, suggested lower figures. The total mattered less than the future mix – more single persons in the population would require more single persons' accommodation.

2 **Inner versus outer city location?** The builders argued that housing must go where people want to live, not where planners think they ought to; and that meant more in outer city areas. Essex preferred to limit their new housing, but London, eager to see regeneration, did not. The local planning organisations and the protest groups preferred to see growth in the Greater London area, arguing that a new town would not help the most deprived sections of the population, who would not be likely to move out. There was some truth in this; however, developers cannot be blamed for the failure of new communities to provide for a wide cross-section of the population. Developers are not unduly wicked, they are building to make a profit and the blame must be placed more on the

111

government for discouraging profitable forms of low-cost rental housing and mixed tenures in new housing schemes.

3 **Land supply.** The builders complained there was inadequate land at affordable prices in London, while surrounding Counties refused to release enough. London and the South East Regional Planning Conference (SERPLAN) argued there was sufficient land in the South East for 600 000 extra dwellings between 1981 and 1991 and the land was already allocated in Structure and Local Plans. Here was a problem of perception: the actual quantity of sites available was less important to the builders than their location and size distribution. Many areas allocated in plans did not meet their marketing requirements nor facilitate comprehensive planning. Brand new settlements in the countryside may be a better solution than haphazard and rather shoddy infill schemes and peripheral estate developments, both from the view of the local authorities, conservation interests and the new households. Thus the argument in favour of new settlements was as much about the management of development pressures in areas of growth, as the opportunity for providing a better life for people living in the inner cities.

4 **The Green Belt.** Although protection of the Green Belt would seem to be a paramount planning goal, the London Green Belt has not been as restrictive as many suppose (Elson, 1986). If additional land is required why should it not be found in the Green Belt, especially if the site is unattractive? The problem is that there is no overall strategic view of where development should be sited in the crowded South East and so the merits of building in the Green Belt are difficult to discuss. When strategic planning was strong, Green Belts around London were complemented by planned New Towns. In the mid-1970s the GLC argued that the New Towns were too successful in drawing people away from London and the policy of planned decentralisation was officially ended. The Tillingham Hall proposal neatly exposed the lack of any strong regional planning framework for decision-making.

Outcome

Nicholas Ridley, Environment Secretary, announced his decision on Tillingham Hall in February, 1987. He rejected the proposal, saying: 'I have concluded that, while recognising the merits of the proposal, there is no justification for allowing this development in the Metropolitan Green Belt.' There was no shortage of housebuilding land available in Essex and even if there had been, the developers had failed to show why the Green Belt should be used for meeting it. However, the concept of private sector new settlements was not ruled out. 'Well conceived schemes of this kind, *in appropriate locations* (author's emphasis) may have a part to play in meeting the demand for new housing, especially when the development meets all or most of the local infrastructure costs and the need for community facilities'.

This example nicely demonstrates the emerging geographical conflicts created by Britain's changing planning process. Wealth-creation goals associated with the changing political economy are ranged against the social and environmental concerns of the State. In this case the 'status quo' is protected. But should it be? And for how long?

Bibliography

There are many different themes relating to the geographical study of planning. The sources listed below provide only a selection of some of the better-known studies which are cited in the text. Articles about planning are to be found in most geographical journals. In addition, *Town and Country Planning* is a lively and topical monthly journal published by the Town and Country Planning Association. *Town Planning Review* and *Built Environment* contain interesting and topical articles about UK planning policy and practice.

General

Cullingworth J.B. 1985, *Town and Country Planning in Britain*, 9th edn, London, Allen and Unwin

Dennis, R. and Clout, H. 1980 *A Social Geography of England and Wales*, Oxford, Pergamon Press

Diamond, D.R. 1977, 'The urban system', in J.W. House, (ed) *The UK Space*, London, Weidenfeld and Nicolson

Fothergill, S and Vincent, J., 1985, *The State of the Nation: An Atlas of Britain in the Eighties*, London, Pan Books Ltd

Freeman, T.W. 1974, *Geography and Planning*, London, Hutchinson

House, J.W. 1973, 'Geographers, decision takers and policy makers', in M. Chisholm and B. Rodgers (eds.), *Studies in Human Geography*, London, Heinemann, pp. 272–305

Jackson, J.N. 1958, *Surveys for Town and Country Planning*, London, Hutchinson

Keeble, L. 1969, *Principles and Practice of Town and Country Planning*, London, Estates Gazette Ltd., p.9

Kivell, P. and Coppock, J.T. 1986, *Geography, Planning and Policy Making*, Norwich, Geo Books

Linton, D.L. 1957, 'Geography and the social revolution', in *Geography*, no. 48, pp. 13–24

Ratcliffe, J. 1981 *An Introduction to Town and Country Planning*, London, Hutchinson

Roberts, M. 1974, *An Introduction to Town Planning Techniques*, London, Hutchinson

Short, J.R. and Kirby, A. 1984, *The Human Geography of Contemporary Britain*, London, Macmillan

Stamp, L.D. 1960, *Applied Geography*, Harmondsworth, Penguin

Willatts, E.C. 1971, 'Planning and geography in the last three decades', *Geographical Journal*, no. 137, pp. 311–338

Woodruffe, B.J. 1976, *Rural Settlement Policies and Plans*, Oxford, Oxford University Press

General texts on the history of planning ideas

Bell, Colin and Rose, 1972, *City Fathers: The early history of town planning in Britain*, London, Penguin

Bruton, M.J. (ed.) 1981, *The Spirit and Purpose of Planning*, London, Hutchinson

Cherry, G.E. 1974, *The Evolution of Town Planning*, Heath and Reach, Leonard Hill

Edwards, A.M. 1981, *The Design of Suburbia*, London, Pembridge Press

Hall, P. 1974, *Urban and Regional Planning*, London, Penguin

Howard, E. 1945, (first published 1903), *Garden Cities of Tomorrow*, London, Faber and Faber

Mumford, L. 1961, *The City in History – Its origins, its transformations and its prospects*, London, Penguin

Selected planning studies and reports of historic interest

Brehenny, M., Hart, D., Hall, P., 1986, *Eastern Promise? Development Prospects for the M11 Corridor*, report prepared for Derrick, Wade and Waters.

Department of Economic Affairs, 1965, *The North West: A Regional Study*, London, HMSO

1969, *The Intermediate Areas, Hunt Report*, Cmnd. 3998, London, HMSO

Royal Commission on the Distribution of the Industrial Population, 1940, *Barlow Report*, Cmnd. 6153, London, HMSO

South East Joint Planning Team, 1970, *Strategic Plan for the South East*, London, Ministry of Housing and Local Government

Short, J.R., Fleming, S. and Witt, S. 1986, *Housebuilding, Planning and Community Action*, London, Routledge and Kegan Paul

Other books and articles which seek to evaluate the wider effects of planning within the context of political economic and social change

Ambrose, P. 1986, *Whatever happened to planning?*, London, Methuen

Caesar, A.A.L. 1964, 'Planning and the geography of Great Britain', *Advancement of Science*, vol. 21

Champion, A., Clegg, K. and Davies, R.L. 1977, *Facts about the New Towns: a Socio-Economic Digest*, Newcastle, Retailing and Planning Associates

Coleman, A. 1985, *Utopia on Trial: Vision and Reality in Planned Housing*, London, Hilary Shipman

Donnisson, D. and Middleton, A. 1987, *Regenerating the Inner City*, London, Routledge and Kegan Paul

Elson, M. 1986, *Green Belts*, London, Allen and Unwin

Fothergill, S. and Gudgin, G. 1982, *Unequal Growth: Urban and Regional Employment Change in the UK*, London, Heinemann

Hall, P., Gracey, H., Drewett, R. and Thomas, R. 1973, *The Containment of Urban England*, 2 vols. London, Allen and Unwin

Harloe, M. 1975, *Swindon: A Town in Transition*, London, Heinemann

Herington, J.M. 1984, *The Outer City*, London, *Paul Chapman Ltd*

Hoare, A.G. 1983, *The Location of Industry in Britain*, Cambridge, Cambridge University Press

House, J.W. 1977, 'Regions and the System', in J.W. House, (ed.) *The UK Space*, London, Weidenfeld and Nicolson

Humphries, I. 1977, 'Power industries', in J.W. House, (ed.) *The UK Space*, London, Weidenfeld and Nicholson

Keeble, D. 1976, *Industrial Location and Planning in the United Kingdom*, London, Methuen

Kirk G. 1980, *Urban Planning in a Capitalist Society*, London, Croom Helm

The geographical analysis of planning areas

Fawcett C.B. 1919, *The Provinces of England*, London, Williams and Norgate

Freeman, T.W. 1968, *Geography and Regional Administration*, Hutchinson, London

Geddes, P. 1915, *Cities in Evolution*, Williams and Margate, 1968 edn., Ernest Bell

Hall, P. 1976, 'The puzzle of the planning regions', *New Society*, I July, 1976, pp. 6–8.

Royal Commission on Local Government in England, 1969, Redcliffe-Maud, *Report Cmnd 4040*, HMSO, 3 vols.

Senior, D. 1966, *The Regional City*, London, Longman

Smailes, A.E. 1944, 'The urban hierarchy in England and Wales', *Geography*, no. 209. pp. 41–51

Spence, N.A. (ed.), 1982, *British Cities: An Analysis of Urban Change*, Oxford, Pergamon Press

National planning policies are interpreted in government circulars which may be obtained in most public libraries and are available from HMSO bookshops

Department of the Environment 1977, *Policy for the Inner Cities*, Cmnd. 6854, London, HMSO
    1980, *Development Control – Policy and Practice*, Circular 22/80, HMSO, London
    1983, *Regional Industrial Development*, Cmnd. 9111, London, HMSO
    1984, *Green Belts*, Circular 15/84, HMSO, London
    1983, *Streamlining the Cities: Government Proposals for Reorganising Local Government in Greater London and the Metropolitan Counties*, Cmnd. 9063, London, HMSO

Local government plans

Copies of the County Structure Plan and Local Plan for your area may be obtained from the relevant County or District Council offices or viewed in the local public library. These plans contain much information of value to local geographical fieldwork and will be essential background reading for the study of planning conflicts.

The politics of geographical conflict

Bennett, R.J. 1982, *Central grants to local government: the political and economic impacts of the Rate Support Grant in England and Wales*, Cambridge, Cambridge University Press

Blowers, A. 1981, *The Limits of Power: The Politics of Local Planning Policy*, Oxford, Pergamon

Cherry, G. 1982, *The Politics of Town Planning*, London, Longman

Church, A. and Hall, J. 1986, 'Discovery of Docklands', *Geographical Magazine* vol. LVIII, no. 12, pp. 632–69

Coates, K. and Silburn, R., 1980, *Beyond the Bulldozer*, Nottingham, University of Nottingham

Fairbrother, N. 1970, *New Lives, New Landscapes*, London, Architectural Press

Gregory, R. 1971, *The Price of Amenity*, London, Macmillan

Herington, J.M. and Hamley, W. 1978, 'The price of coal in Belvoir,' *Geographical Magazine*, no. 50, February, 1978, Vol. 1, no. 5, pp. 307–314.

Kirby, A.M. 1982, *The Politics of Location*, London, Methuen

Lowe, P. and Goyder, J. 1983, *Environmental Groups in Politics*, London, George Allen and Unwin

Munton, R. 1986, 'Green Belts: an end of an era?' *Geography*, vol. 71, no. 312, pp. 206–214

Simmons, M., 1985, 'Motorways and development: the case of the M25 London Orbital', *The Planner*, Vol. 71, no. 2, pp. 55–58

Shiller, R. 1986, 'Retail decentralisation – the coming of the third wave', *The Planner*, July, 1986, no. 72, p. 7.

Pahl, R.E. 1975, *Whose City? And further essays on Urban Society* London, Penguin

Sim, D. 1984, 'Urban deprivation: not just the inner city', *Area*, vol. 16, no. 4, pp. 299–306

Town and Country Planning Association, 1986, *Whose Responsibility? Reclaiming the Inner Cities*, London, HMSO

Town and Country Planning Association 1987, *North–South Divide, A New Deal for Britain's Regions*, London, TCPA

Townsend, A. 1980, 'Unemployment geography and the government's new regional aid', *Area*, vol. 12. no. 1.

Willmott, Y. and Young, M. 1957, *Family and Kinship in East London*, London, Routledge and Kegan Paul

Index